Michael Price

Office 2010

In easy steps is an imprint of In Easy Steps Limited
4 Chapel Court · 42 Holly Walk · Leamington Spa
Warwickshire · United Kingdom · CV32 4YS
www.ineasysteps.com

Reprinted 2011

Notice of Liability
Every effort has been made to ensure that this book contains accurate
and current information. However, In Easy Steps Limited and the
author shall not be liable for any loss or damage suffered by readers
as a result of any information contained herein.

Trademarks
Microsoft® and Windows® are registered trademarks of Microsoft
Corporation. All other trademarks are acknowledged as belonging to
their respective companies.

In Easy Steps Limited supports The Forest Stewardship Council (FSC),
the leading international forest certification organisation. All our titles
that are printed on Greenpeace approved FSC certified paper carry the
FSC logo.

MIX
Paper from
responsible sources
FSC® C020837

FSC
www.fsc.org

Printed and bound in the United Kingdom

ISBN 978-1-84078-398-8

Contents

4 Calculations 67

5 Manage Data 85

6 Presentations 107

7   Office Extras   127

8   Email   145

9   Time Management   165

10 Manage Files 187

11 Up to Date and Secure 203

12 Where Next? 219

Index 233

1 Introducing Office 2010

This chapter discusses the latest version of Microsoft Office, with its ribbon style of user interface. It identifies the range of editions, and outlines the requirements for installation. Also covered are the process of starting applications, features such as Preview and Save, used by all Office applications, Office document types and compatibility with the older versions of applications.

Microsoft Office 2010

Microsoft Office is a productivity suite of applications that share common features and approaches. There have been numerous versions, including Office 95, Office 97, Office 2000, Office XP (also called Office 2002), Office 2003 and Office 2007. The latest version, released in June 2010, is Microsoft Office 2010.

There are various editions, with particular combinations of applications. The Home and Student edition contains:

- Excel 2010   Spreadsheet and data manager
- PowerPoint 2010   Presentations and slide shows
- OneNote 2010   For taking notes
- Word 2010   Text editor and word processor
- Office Tools   Diagnostics and image utilities

The Home and Business edition of Office contains all of the applications in the Home and Student edition, plus:

- Outlook 2010   Electronic mail and diary

The Professional edition of Office contains all that found in Home and Business edition, plus two additional applications:

- Access 2010   Database manager
- Publisher 2010   Professional document creation

There's also a Professional Academic edition, which contains the same applications as the Professional edition, but at a preferred price for qualified users.

To illustrate the relative costs for these editions, recommended prices in the USA (and the numbers of licenses included) are:

Edition	Boxed		Key Card	
Home and Student	$149	(3)	$119	(1)
Home and Business	$279	(2)	$199	(1)
Professional	$499	(2)	$349	(1)
Professional Academic	$ 99	(2)	n/a	

If you run 64-bit Windows 7 or Windows Vista, there is a 64-bit version of Office 2010 available. However, you should still run the 32-bit version, unless you have very large Excel spreadsheets.

Don't forget

New PCs may come with Office 2010 Starter edition, which contains Lite versions of Word and Excel. There are also Standard and Professional Plus editions for businesses, but these are not available in retail packages. See page 220 for details of all the editions of Office 2010.

Microsoft®
Office
2010

Don't forget

There's no upgrade pricing for Office 2010 editions, but there is a key card price for pre-installed or downloaded copies. This is for a single PC only, unlike the boxed editions, which include 2 licenses (or 3 for the Home and Student).

Ribbon Technology

Whichever edition you have, the most notable feature of Office 2010 is the graphical user interface based on the Ribbon. This replaces the menus and toolbars that were the essence of previous versions of Office.

Hot tip

This result-oriented user interface was first introduced in Office 2007, and now appears in all the applications in Office 2010.

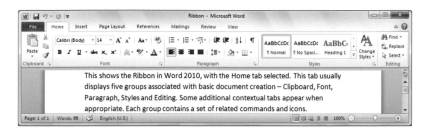

This shows the Ribbon in Word 2010, with the Home tab selected. This tab usually displays five groups associated with basic document creation – Clipboard, Font, Paragraph, Styles and Editing. Some additional contextual tabs appear when appropriate. Each group contains a set of related commands and icons.

The Ribbon contains command buttons and icons, organized in a set of tabs, each containing groups of commands associated with specific functions. The purpose is to make the relevant features more intuitive, and more readily available. This allows you to concentrate on the tasks you want to perform rather than the details of how you will carry out the activities.

Some tabs appear only when certain objects are selected. These are known as contextual tabs and provide functions that are specific to the selected object. For example, when you select an inserted image, the Picture Tools Format tab and its groups are displayed.

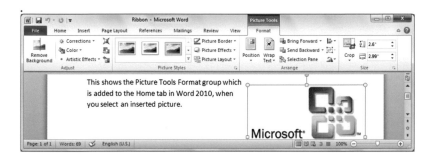

This shows the Picture Tools Format group which is added to the Home tab in Word 2010, when you select an inserted picture.

Don't forget

You can rename and change the order of the default tabs and groups, and you can create your own custom tabs and add groups to the ribbon. See page 44 for an example.

The Ribbon based user interface also features extended ScreenTips that can contain images and links to more help, as well as text. The tips are displayed when you move the mouse pointer over a command, they describe what the commands do, and give keyboard shortcuts.

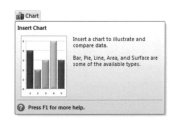

What's Needed

To use Microsoft Office 2010, you will need at least the following components in your computer:

- 500 MHz processor

- 256 MB memory

- 3.0 GB available disk space

- CD-ROM or DVD drive

- 1024×768 resolution monitor

- Windows 7, Windows Vista (+SP1), or Windows XP (+SP2)

Some functions impose more stringent requirements, for example:

- 512 MB memory for Outlook Instant Search

- 1.0 GB memory for Word grammar and contextual spelling

- Internet connection for online help

If your computer is running Windows 7, you'll find that the system specifications already meet or exceed requirements for Office 2010. You'll also find that the Office 2010 user interface coordinates well with the visual style of Windows 7 and Aero.

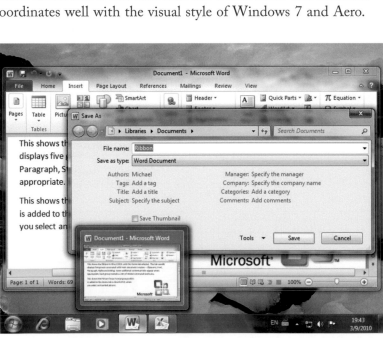

Installing Office 2010

If you've purchased a new copy of Office 2010, you will need to install it onto your computer. Insert the supplied CD or DVD, enter the 25 character product key, and accept the terms and conditions. Follow the prompts to complete the installation.

1 Select Install Now to accept the default settings

2 Select Customize to choose how items are installed, then click a component and choose Run all from My Computer to include all the extras for that item

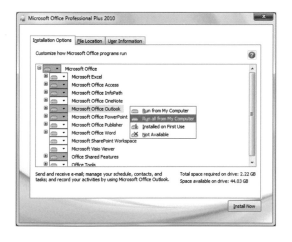

3 Select Not Available to exclude the selected component

Hot tip

If you have an older version of Office, you may be offered the option to upgrade the existing installation.

Don't forget

Click the Microsoft Office entry and select Run all from My Computer, to install extras for all of the components.

Start an Application

Hot tip

This shows Windows 7. However, the same shortcuts are added to the Windows Vista or the Windows XP Start Menu.

When you have installed Office 2010, a new folder of shortcuts will be added to the Start Menu.

1 Select Start, All Programs

2 Select Microsoft Office to display all the installed applications

3 Select Microsoft Office Tools to display the various utilities

4 Select the application that you wish to run, for example Word 2010

When you start any Office application, you are reminded that you must activate your installation to fully enable all the features.

Beware

If you choose not to activate immediately, you can run the software for a period of 30 days, before it makes features unavailable.

5 You can activate your copy of Office 2010 over the Internet or by telephone

Don't forget

Activating an application in Office activates all the other applications in the suite at the same time.

The Application Window

When you start an Office application, such as Excel, PowerPoint or Word, the program window is displayed with a blank document named Book1, Presentation1, or Document1, respectively. Using Word as an example, the parts of the application window include:

BackStage (File tab)　Quick Access toolbar　Document name　Tabs

Minimize/Restore/Close

Help button

Ribbon

Commands and icons (display lists or galleries)

Launch button (shows dialog box)

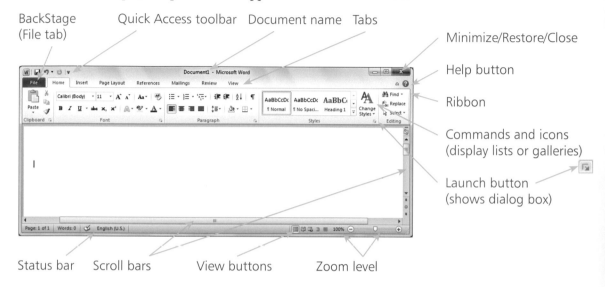

Status bar　Scroll bars　View buttons　Zoom level

Applications like Access and Publisher don't open a blank document, but open in the BackStage view instead and offer a set of predefined layouts. For Publisher, these include brochures, business cards, calendars and labels, as well as blank documents.

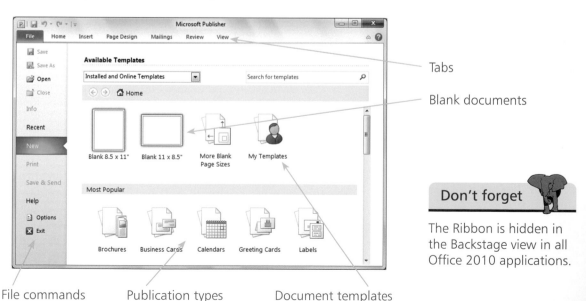

Tabs

Blank documents

File commands　Publication types　Document templates

Don't forget

The Ribbon is hidden in the Backstage view in all Office 2010 applications.

Live Preview

With the Ribbon interface, you can see the full effect of formatting options on your document, such as fonts and styles, by simply pointing to the proposed change. For example, to see font formatting changes:

1 Highlight the text that you may wish to change, then select the Home tab

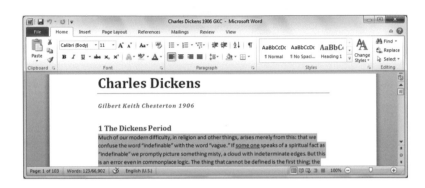

Don't forget

In previous versions, you would be shown a preview of the new font or style using a small amount of sample text.

2 Click the arrow next to the Font box and move the mouse pointer over the fonts you'd like to preview

Don't forget

The selected text is temporarily altered to show the font (or the font size, color or highlight) you point to.

3 Click the font you want to actually apply the change to the text, or press Escape to finish viewing font options

4 Similarly, you can preview the alternatives provided for the Font Size, the Font Color, and the Text Highlight Color options

Live Preview is available for paragraph format options (e.g. bullets, numbering, and shading) and for styles.

1 Highlight the text that you may wish to change, then select the Home tab

Don't forget

This facility is not available in Excel, which does not offer the Paragraph group.

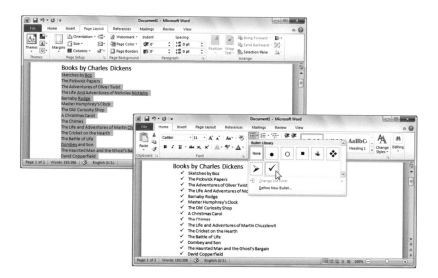

Hot tip

The option will be previewed for the paragraph where the pointer is currently located, if no text has been selected.

2 Display the list of paragraph options, and move the mouse pointer over any that you want to preview

3 Display the list of styles (with no text selected) and preview the complete document in a variety of styles

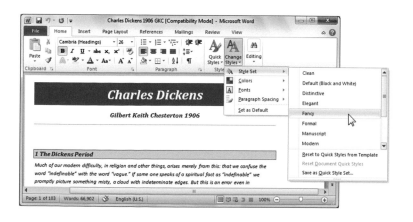

Don't forget

You can turn off Live Preview for individual applications. Click the File tab, select the application Options command, click General, and then clear the Enable Live Preview box.

15

Save the Document

You'll use the appropriate commands on the Ribbon for each application, to create and amend the application document. You should save the document periodically, to avoid the possibility of losing the work you've done.

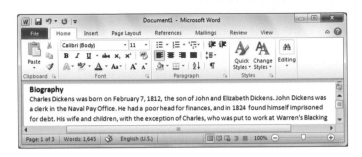

1 Click the File tab and select Save

2 For a document not yet named and saved, the Save As dialog opens so you can provide a name (or use the suggested name)

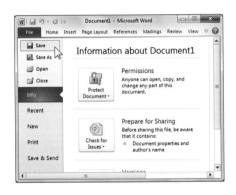

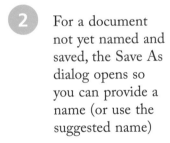 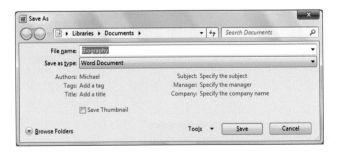

3 On subsequent Saves, the document will then be written to disk without any further action needed

4 To save the document under a new name, select the File tab, and then select Save As

Working With the Ribbon

The Ribbon takes up a significant amount of the window space, especially when you have a lower-resolution display. To hide it:

1 Click Minimize the Ribbon, or Right-click the tab bar and select Minimize the Ribbon

2 The File tab, Quick Access toolbar, and tab bar will still be displayed while the Ribbon is minimized

3 The Ribbon reappears temporarily when you click one of the tabs, so you can select the required command

4 Alternatively, press and release the Alt key to display keyboard shortcuts for the tabs

5 Press Alt + shortcut key, for example Alt+P, to select Page Layout, and display the Ribbon and shortcuts for that tab

Quick Access Toolbar

The Quick Access toolbar contains a set of commands that are independent of the selected tab. There are four buttons initially:

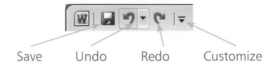

Save   Undo   Redo   Customize

1 Click the Save button to write the current contents of the application document to the disk drive

2 Click Undo to reverse the last action, click Redo to re-apply, and click the arrow to select several actions to undo

3 Click the Customize button to add or remove icons, using the list of popular commands

4 Click More Commands to display the full list of commands, then add and remove entries as desired

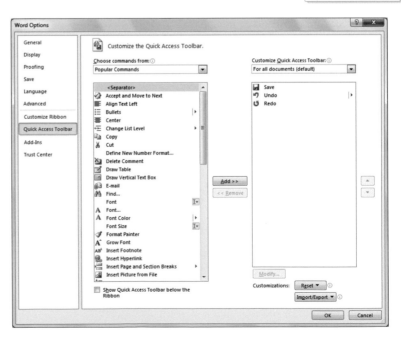

18

Office Document Types

The objects you create using the Office applications will be office documents of various types, including:

- Formatted text and graphics   Word document
- Flyers and brochures   Publisher publication
- Spreadsheets and data lists   Excel worksheet
- Presentations and slide shows   PowerPoint presentation

Each item will be a separate file. By default, these will be saved in the Documents library for your username (logon ID).

1   To show the entries currently stored in your folder, click Start and select Documents from the list

Hot tip

The Documents library consists of the Documents folder for the current user, and the Public (shared) Documents folder.

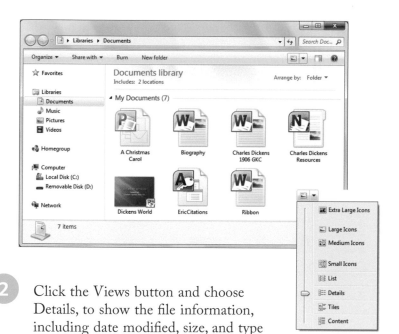

Don't forget

You can specify a different folder, or subfolder, for particular sets of documents.

2   Click the Views button and choose Details, to show the file information, including date modified, size, and type

Note that, in some applications, groups of related items will be stored together in a specially structured file. For example:

- Data tables, queries and reports   Access database
- Messages, contacts and tasks   Outlook folders
- Notes and reminders   OneNote folders

File Extensions

To see the file extensions associated with these document types:

1 Click the Organize button, then select Folder and search options

Organize ▼

Folder and search options

2 Click the View tab

3 Search through the list of Advanced settings to locate and clear the box for "Hide extensions for known file types"

4 Click OK to apply the change to all folders

5 The file type will be shown, along with the file name, whichever folder view you choose

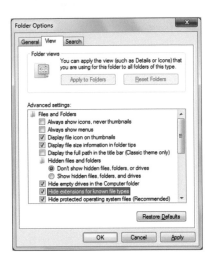

Compatibility Mode

Office 2010 will open documents created in previous versions of Office applications, for example .doc (Word) or .xls (Excel).

1 Click the File tab and select Open, then click the down arrow for document type to list the types supported

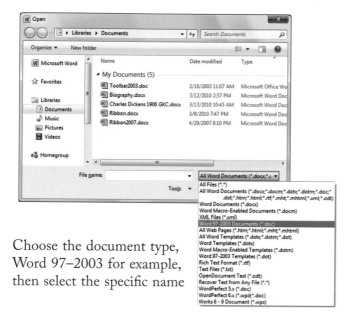

2 Choose the document type, Word 97–2003 for example, then select the specific name

Compatibility Mode

3 Documents created in previous versions (including .docx files from Word 2007) are opened in Compatibility Mode

Convert to Office 2010

If you have opened a document in Compatibility Mode, you can convert it to the standard Office 2010 format.

1 Select the File tab button and click the Convert button

2 Click OK to confirm that you want to convert the document, and the compatibility restriction will be removed

3 To replace the original file, select File and then Save, or click the Save button on the Quick Access toolbar

4 To retain the original while creating a new file in Office 2010 format, select File, then Save As, and then click Save

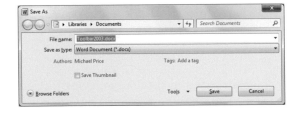

Save to Web

Save your Office 2010 document online, in the Windows Live SkyDrive, a central location where you and others can view and edit documents in the browser. To save the document

1 Open the document in the Office 2010 application

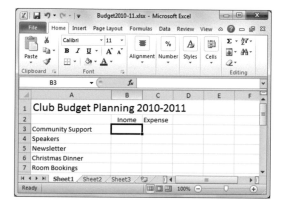

2 Select the File tab, and, in the BackStage view, click Save & Send and then click Save to Web

3 Click Sign In, enter your Windows Live ID (email address) and your password, and then click OK

Hot tip

You can save Word, Excel, PowerPoint, and OneNote documents in SkyDrive, and access them using Office Web Apps (see page 228 for details).

Hot tip

If you use Hotmail, Messenger, or Xbox Live, you already have a Windows Live ID. If you don't have one, click Sign up to create a new Windows Live ID.

...cont'd

4 Select a Windows Live SkyDrive folder and click Save As

Click New Folder to create a folder on SkyDrive, for your use or to share with others.

5 Type a name for your file and click Save.

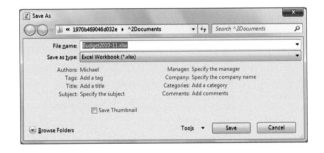

6 Visit skydrive.live.com to view your files and folders.

Using SkyDrive, you can send a link rather than an attachment, and maintain a single copy of the document that others can view and update.

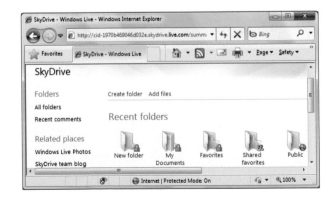

2 Create Word Documents

This covers the basics of word processing, using the Word application in Office 2010. It covers entering, selecting and copying text, saving and autosaving, and proofing the text. It looks at the use of styles to structure the document, and at adding document features, such as pictures, columns, and word counts. It also discusses ways of creating tables, the use of Paste Special, and the facilities for printing.

Create a Word Document

1 Right-click an empty space in a folder (e.g. Documents) and select New, Microsoft Word Document

2 A blank document, temporarily named Document1, will be created when you start Word (see page 12)

3 If Word is open, select the File tab, click Open, choose the Blank document, and click the Create button

Enter Text

1 Click on the page and type the text that you want. If the text is longer than a single line, Word automatically starts the new line for you

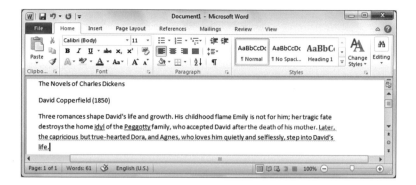

Hot tip

You can copy and paste text from other sources, such as web pages. Use Paste Options (see page 29) to avoid copying styles and formats along with the text.

2 Press Enter when you need to start a new line or paragraph

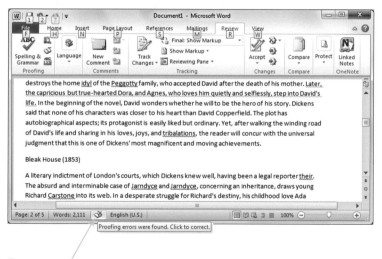

Don't forget

You may see blue, wavy underscores to indicate contextual spelling errors (misused words), such as Their in place of There.

3 Proofing errors may be detected, as indicated by the wavy underscores – red (spelling) or green (grammar).

4 Click the button on the status bar to correct them one by one, or correct them all at the same time, when you've finished typing the whole document (see page 31)

Select and Copy Text

It's necessary to select text for many purposes in Word, so it's not surprising that there are numerous ways to select just the amount of text you require, using the mouse or the keyboard, as preferred. To select the entire document, use one of these options:

1 Select the Home tab, click Select in the Editing group, and then click the Select All command

2 Move the mouse pointer to the left of any text until it turns into a right–pointing arrow, then triple-click

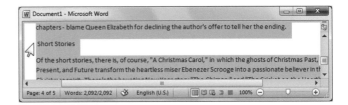

3 Press the shortcut keys Ctrl+A

There are many mouse and keyboard options for selecting a piece of text in the body of the document. For example:

1 Double-click anywhere in a word to select it

2 Hold down Ctrl and click anywhere in a sentence to select the whole sentence

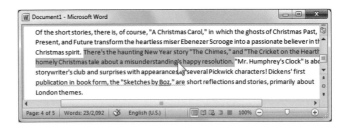

3 To select a portion of text, click at the start, hold down the left mouse button and drag the pointer over the text

You can use text selection in combination with the Clipboard tools, to copy or move parts of the text. For example:

1 Select a section of text using the mouse

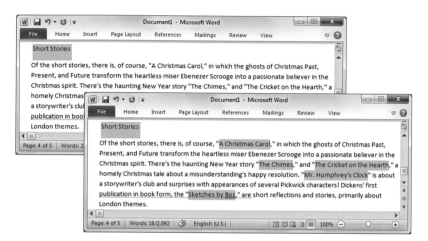

2 Hold down the Ctrl key and select additional pieces of text, select Home and click the Copy button in the Clipboard group

3 Click the position where the text is required, then select Home and click the Paste button

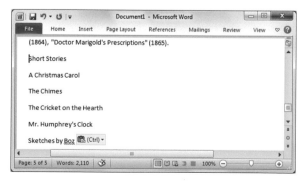

4 If you've copied several pieces of text, each piece appears on a separate line, so you will need to delete the end-of-line characters to join them up

Save the Document

When you are building a document, Word will periodically save a copy of the document, just in case a problem arises. This minimizes the amount of text you may need to re-enter. This feature is known as AutoRecover. To check the settings:

1 Click the File tab, select the Word Options and click the Save command

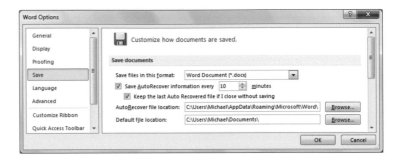

By default, Word will save AutoRecover information every ten minutes, but you can change the frequency.

To make an immediate save of your document:

1 Click the Save button on the Quick Access toolbar

2 The first time, you'll be prompted to confirm the location, the file name, and the document type that you want to use

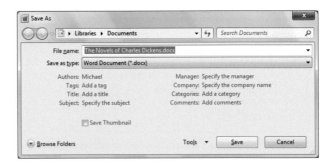

3 On subsequent saves, the document on the hard disk will be updated immediately, without further interaction

30

Correct Proofing Errors

When you've entered all the text, you can correct proofing errors.

1 Press Ctrl+Home to go to the start of the document, then select the Review tab and click Spelling & Grammar

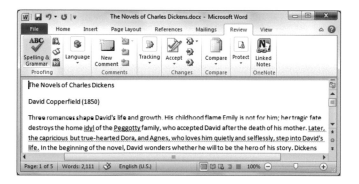

2 For spelling errors, choose the correct word and then click Change

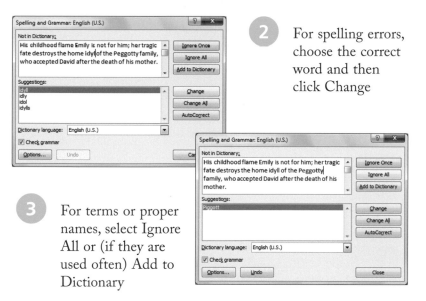

3 For terms or proper names, select Ignore All or (if they are used often) Add to Dictionary

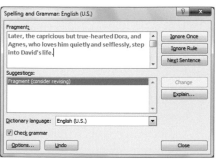

4 Grammar and style errors are less definitive, you must decide about each suggestion on its merits

Change Proofing Settings

1 Click the File tab, select Word Options, and then select the Proofing command

2 Some settings, such as Ignore words in uppercase and Flag repeated words, apply to all the Office applications

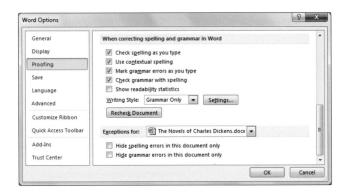

3 Some settings, such as Check spelling as you type and Mark grammar errors as you type, are specific to the particular Office application, in this case, Word

The suggestions that will be offered include:

seen
see
Where or Here

4 The contextual spelling checker in Word identifies words that are spelled correctly, but used in the wrong context, and suggests alternative words that might be more appropriate

Apply Styles

1 Click the main heading and select Style Heading 1

Don't forget

You can change the style for parts of the text to suit the particular contents, using the Styles group on the Home tab.

2 Click on one of the subsidiary headings and select Heading 2

Hot tip

Click the down arrow to show the next row of styles

3 Click in the text paragraph and select No Spacing

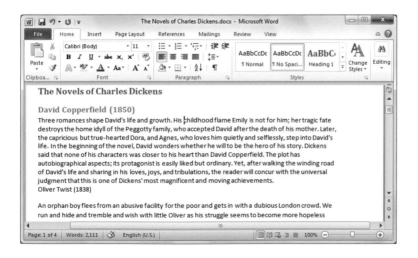

Don't forget

Apply these two styles to other headings and paragraphs. To repeat a style, select an example, double-click the Format Painter icon, and then click each similar item in turn.

Outline View

When you have structured the document using headings, you can view it as an outline:

1 Select the View tab and click the Outline button, to switch to Outline view and enable the Outlining tab

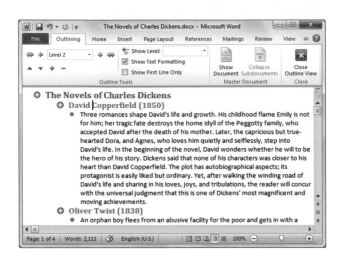

2 In the Outline Tools group, click the box labelled Show First Line Only, so that you can see more entries at once

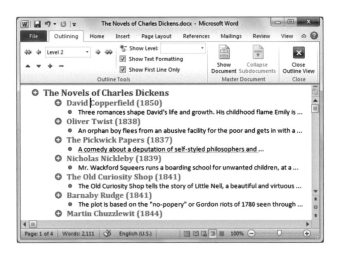

This makes it easier for you to identify any entries that are out of order. In this example, the entries for David Copperfield and Oliver Twist are out of chronological sequence.

Outline view also makes it easy for you to reposition selected entries.

1 Click the arrow next to Show Level, and choose Level 2

2 Click an entry, e.g. David Copperfield, and click the down arrow to move it

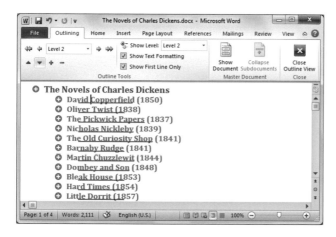

3 The selected entry, with all its subsidiary levels and text, will move one row for each click of the arrow button

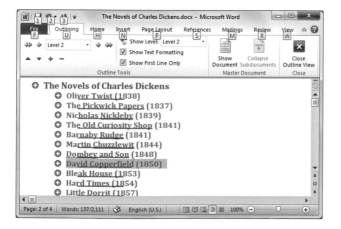

4 Repeat to reposition another entry, e.g. Oliver Twist

Don't forget

This will display the selected level, and all higher levels.

Don't forget

The Outline tools also provide buttons that allow you to promote or demote selected entries.

Hot tip

You can click the + symbol next to an entry to select it, and then drag it to the required location.

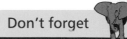

35

Insert a Picture

1 Position the typing cursor at the location where the item is required, inserting a blank line if desired

2 Select the Insert tab and click the appropriate icon or command, for example Picture (in the Illustrations group)

3 Locate the file for the picture, and click the Insert button

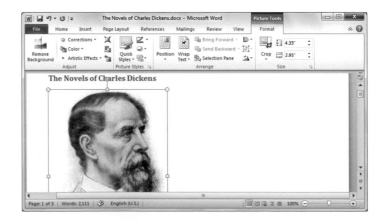

You can adjust the position of the picture on the page of text.

1 Click the Position button in the Arrangements group and move the pointer over the buttons

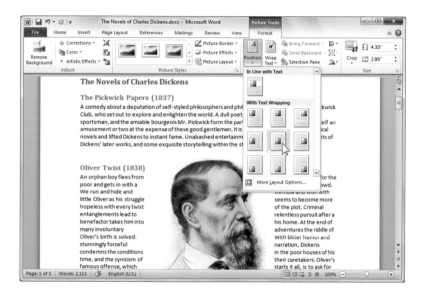

Don't forget

The Format tab allows you to change the size, select a frame, and adjust the brightness, contrast, and color of the picture.

2 A live preview will be displayed. Click the appropriate button for the position you prefer

3 Click the up or down arrow on the height, to adjust the size of the picture. The width is changed proportionally

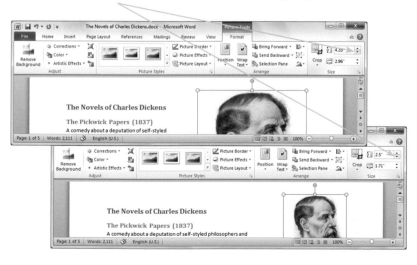

Hot tip

Having selected a position, you can click and drag the picture to make fine adjustments.

Don't forget

The original proportions of the picture will be maintained, when you make changes to the height or width.

Page Layout

The Page Layout tab allows you to control how the document contents are placed on the page, by just clicking one of the function command buttons in the Page Setup group.

Hot tip

To display the vertical and horizontal rulers, as shown here, select the View tab and then click the Ruler box, from the Show group.

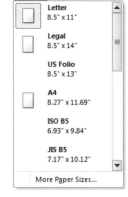

1 Click the Orientation button to select Portrait or Landscape

2 Click the Size button to select the paper size from the list, or click More Paper Sizes to show other choices, including Custom Size

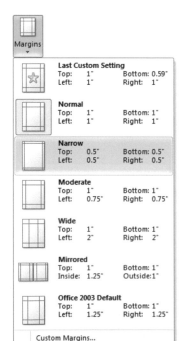

Don't forget

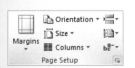

You can also press the arrow on the Page Setup group bar to display the Page Setup dialog.

3 Click the Margins button to choose one of the predefined setups, Narrow for example, or click Custom Margins to display the Page Setup dialog, and then enter the specific values

Display in Columns

1 Select the text you wish to put into columns, click the Page Layout tab, and then select Columns from Page Setup

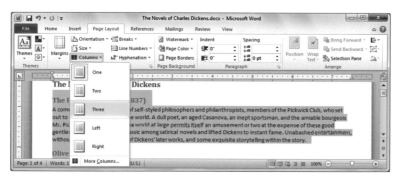

Hot tip

Leave all of the text unselected if you wish to apply the columns to the whole document.

2 Choose the number of columns required

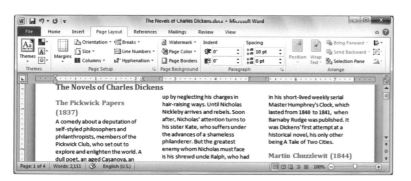

Hot tip

Choose Justify for the paragraph text, to help give the document the appearance of newspaper columns. Choose Center, for the title text to place it over the three columns.

3 Click in the body text, select the Home tab, click Select, Select Text with Similar Formatting, and click the Justify button

Don't forget

Select File, Options, Advanced, and choose to Keep track of formatting, to enable Select text with Similar Formatting.

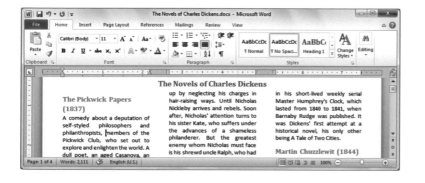

Word Count

If you are preparing a document for a publication, such as a club magazine, you may need to keep track of the number of words:

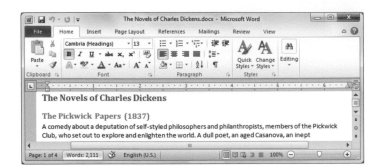

1 View the word count for the document on the status bar

2 Click the word count to display the detailed counts for pages, paragraphs, lines, and characters

For a fuller analysis of the contents of the document:

1 Select File, Options, Proofing, then Show readability statistics

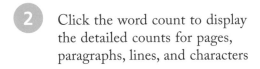

2 Select the Review tab, then click the Spelling & Grammar button in the Proofing group and check the document

3 After the spelling check is completed, the document statistics are displayed

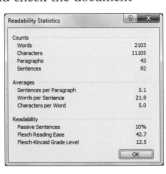

Create a Table

To specify a table in your document:

1 Click the point where you want the table, then click the Insert tab, and select Table

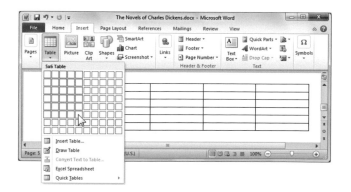

Hot tip

You'll see previews of the indicated table sizes as you move the pointer across the Insert Table area.

2 Move the pointer over the Insert Table area to select the number of rows and columns, then click to confirm

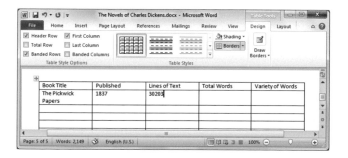

Don't forget

Press the arrow keys to navigate around the table. Click and drag a separator line to adjust the width of a column.

3 Enter the required contents. Press the Tab key to move to the next cell in the table

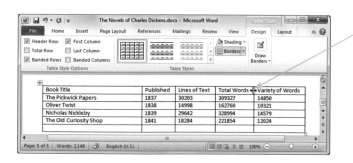

Convert Text to Table

Hot tip

Select Home, then click the Show/Hide button in the Paragraph group to display tabs and paragraph marks. Two consecutive tabs indicate an empty cell. Paragraph marks separate the rows.

If you already have the text that's needed for the table, perhaps taken from another document, you can convert the text into a table.

1 Make sure that the cell entries are separated by a tab mark, or some other unique character

Don't forget

Select Autofit to contents, to adjust the column widths to match the data in those cells.

2 Highlight the text, select the Insert tab, and then click Table, Convert Text to Table

3 Specify your particular separation character and then click OK

4 The table will be created with the data inserted into the relevant cells

Don't forget

The cursor must be in the table area to display the Table Tools tab. Select Layout to apply operations, such as insert, delete, merge, and align.

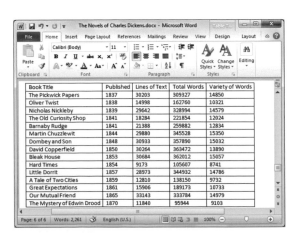

Book Title	Published	Lines of Text	Total Words	Variety of Words
The Pickwick Papers	1837	30203	309327	14850
Oliver Twist	1838	14998	162760	10321
Nicholas Nickleby	1839	29642	328994	14579
The Old Curiosity Shop	1841	18284	221854	12024
Barnaby Rudge	1841	21388	259882	12834
Martin Chuzzlewit	1844	29880	345528	15350
Dombey and Son	1848	30933	357890	15032
David Copperfield	1850	30264	363472	13890
Bleak House	1853	30684	362012	15057
Hard Times	1854	9173	105607	8741
Little Dorrit	1857	28973	344932	14786
A Tale of Two Cities	1859	12810	138150	9732
Great Expectations	1861	15906	189173	10733
Our Mutual Friend	1865	33143	333784	14979
The Mystery of Edwin Drood	1870	11840	95944	9103

Paste Special

To copy the text without including its formatting and graphics:

1 Highlight the text you want, then right-click the selected area and click the Copy command

2 Click in the document where the text is to appear, select the Home tab, and then click the arrow below the Paste button

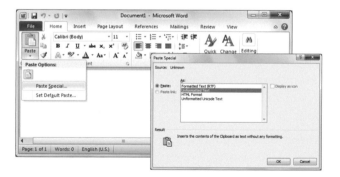

3 Click Paste Special and choose Paste, Unformatted Text

43

Hot tip

When you copy information from other documents, or from web pages, the text may include graphics, formatting, and colors that are inappropriate for your document.

Beware

Graphical information won't be copied, even if it has the appearance of text (as with the Dickens Fast Facts title being copied for this example).

Don't forget

The copied text will inherit the format of that part of the document you clicked before carrying out the paste operation.

Print Document

To print a document from within Word:

 1   Click the File tab and select Print (or press Ctrl+P)

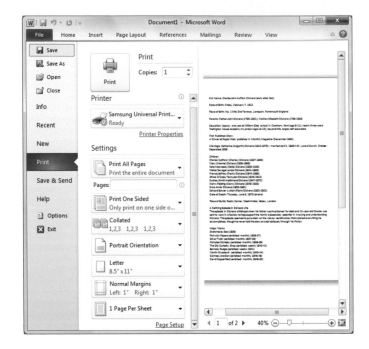

2   From here, you can preview the document, using the zoom slider, the scroll bars, and the page change buttons

3   Select the specific printer to use

4   Choose the pages to be printed, and adjust other settings, such as the paper size and the margins

5   Specify the number of copies, then click the Print button

Quick Print

You can add a Print group and a Quick Print button to one of the tabs on the ribbon, to get an immediate print of the current document, using the default settings.

3 Complex Documents

Microsoft Word can be used to create and edit more complex documents, such as booklets and brochures. This chapter covers importing text, inserting illustrations, creating tables of contents, and illustrations. It shows how templates can be used to help create documents. It also introduces Publisher, the Office application that is specifically designed for desktop publishing.

Start a Booklet

To illustrate some of the facilities available for creating and organizing complex documents, we'll go through the process of importing and structuring the text for a booklet. In this example, we use the text for *A Christmas Carol* by Charles Dickens.

1 Start by typing the book title, author, and chapter names

2 Set the language. This is a United Kingdom book, so press Ctrl+A to select the text, click the Language button on the status bar, and pick English (UK)

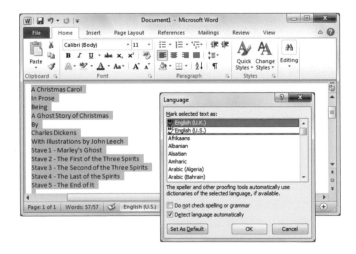

3 Click Save, on the Quick Access toolbar, and provide a name for the document, or accept the suggested name

Choose Page Arrangement

Before adding more text, set the paper size and the margins.

1 Select the Page Layout tab, and click Size to choose paper size, e.g. Letter

2 Click Margins and choose the Custom Margins option

3 From the Page Setup dialog, in the Pages section, select Multiple pages, Book fold

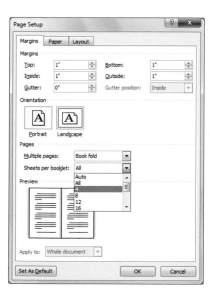

4 Specify the number of sheets per booklet (in multiples of 4 up to 40) or choose All to assemble the document as a single booklet

Hot tip

For a book or brochure, you may want to arrange the pages in the form of booklets.

Don't forget

The orientation changes to landscape, and you get four pages of the document on each piece of paper (printed on both sides). A four-sheet booklet, for example, would be printed as:

Front

4 1

Back

2 3

Create the Structure

1 Highlight the text for the chapter titles

2 Click the Home tab and select Quick Styles, Heading 1

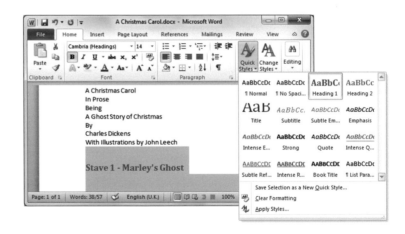

3 With the chapter titles still selected, click the Center button in the Paragraph group

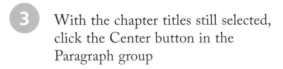

4 To replace hyphens with line breaks in the chapter titles, click the Editing button and select Replace, again with the text for the chapter titles selected

5 In the Find what box, type a hyphen, with a space either side, that is " - " (without the quotation marks)

6 In the Replace with box, type "^l" (the control code for a manual line break), then select Replace All

7 This changes all the occurrences in the selected text. Click No to skip the remainder of the document, to avoid changing hyphens elsewhere in the text

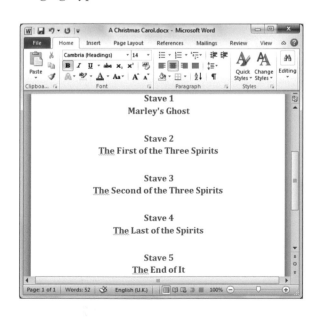

Import Text

1 Click just to the right of the Stave 1 title, and select Insert, Page Break, to start the chapter on a new page

Hot tip

Type paragraphs of text, insert text from a file, or copy and paste text from a file, if you just want part of the contents.

2 Click the page, just past the end of the title, and press Enter to add a new blank line (in Body Text style)

3 Select Insert, click Insert Object, and choose Text from File

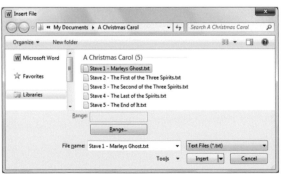

Don't forget

This option was known as Insert File in previous versions of Word. It allows you to transfer the contents from various file types, including Word, web, and text.

4 Locate the file holding the required text and click Insert

5 Click OK to select the appropriate encoding, if prompted

Hot tip

Step 5 is only required when the system needs your help in interpreting the imported text.

The text will be copied to the document at the required location.

51

Repeat steps 1 to 5 for each chapter in the book. To adjust styles:

1 Click anywhere in the new text, click the Home tab, then click Select and choose Select Text with Similar Formatting

Hot tip

The inserted text may not have the format you require, but you can change all the inserted text in a single operation.

2 Select your preferred style, e.g. Normal, No Spacing

3 All the text you inserted into the document will be converted to the selected style

Insert Illustrations

1 Find the location for an illustration. For example, select Home, click Find, and enter a search term, such as Figure:

Hot tip

The sample text has the titles for the illustrations at the required locations, in the form of:
Figure: Title of illustration

Don't forget

You can insert pictures from image files of all the usual types, including bitmap, jpeg (photos), and gif (web graphics).

52

2 For each location, select the Insert tab and click Picture

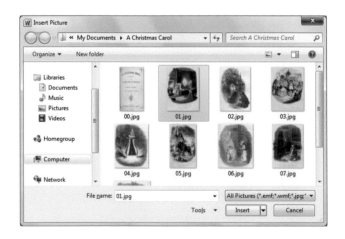

3 Locate the file containing the required illustration and click Insert, the picture is then inserted into the document, in line with the text, where you can adjust its position

Add Captions

1 From the Reference tab, select Insert Caption and click OK

2 After the automatic number, type a colon : and click OK, to join this to the picture title

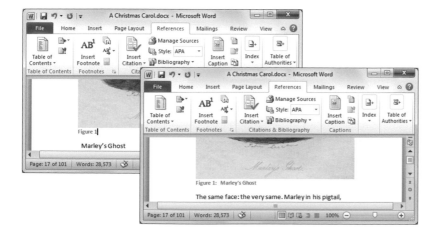

Don't forget

Repeat these two sets of steps to insert a picture and a caption for each of the figures in the book.

Don't forget

If the document doesn't already contain the title for the illustration, type it after the automatic number in the Caption box (or directly into the document after Figure #).

Hot tip

The captions that you create are used to create a table of illustrations (see page 56).

Table of Contents

When you have formatted text within the document with heading levels, you can use these to create and maintain a contents list.

1 Click the Page Number button on the Status bar, type the number 2 and click Go To, then Close, to show that page

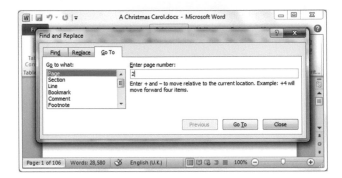

Hot tip

You can prefix the number with + or - to go forward or back for the specified number of pages.

2 Select the Insert tab and click Blank Page in the Pages group, to insert a blank page for the contents list

Don't forget

Select Home, and click Align Text Left in the paragraph group, before selecting the Table of Contents button.

3 Go to the new page 2, select the References tab, and click the Table of Contents button

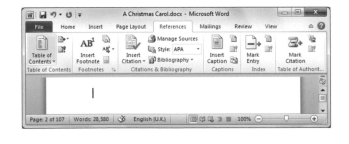

4 Choose the type of table that you want, for example Automatic Table 1 (with Contents as the title)

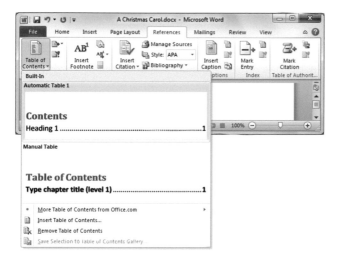

Hot tip

This type of table will use heading levels 1, 2 and 3 to generate the table. You can also build a table using custom styles, or based on manually selected text.

5 The table of contents is inserted. When it is selected, the entries are greyed, to indicate field codes (action items)

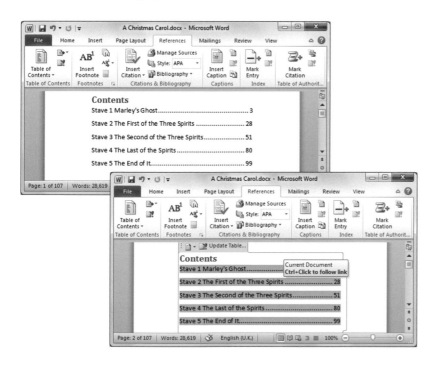

Beware

The table of contents must be updated to show any changes to the heading-text content, or to the page-number value.

Don't forget

When you hover the mouse pointer over an entry in the table, with the shift key pressed, you'll have a link to the associated section of the document.

Table of Illustrations

1 Go to the start of chapter 1 and insert another blank page, this time for a list of illustrations

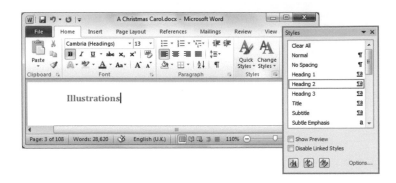

2 On the new page, type Illustrations, select the Home tab, the arrow to expand the Styles group, and Heading 2

3 Press Enter to add a blank line, then, on the References tab, click Insert Table of Figures

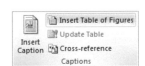

4 Clear the box Include label and number, if desired

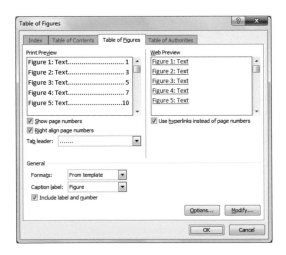

5 Click OK to insert the table of figures

6 The table of figures is similar to the table of contents

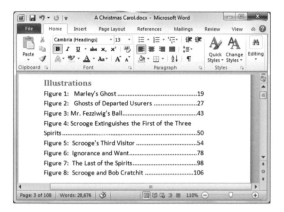

Don't forget

There's no heading included, so any heading required must be provided separately, in this case, Illustrations.

7 Click the table to see field codes and links to the figures

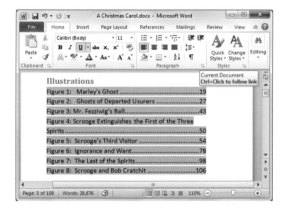

8 Highlight the whole table and select Toggle Field Codes

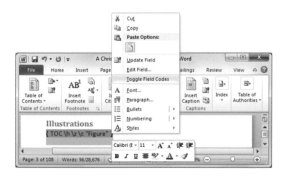

Don't forget

The format of the field code for the table of figures indicates that it is actually a TOC (table of contents) based on the Figure label.

Insert Preface

1 Go to page 2 (the contents page) and insert a blank page for the book preface

2 On the new page, type Preface, select the Home tab, the arrow to expand the Styles group, and Heading 2

3 Press Enter and insert text from a file (see page 50), or type the text for the preface

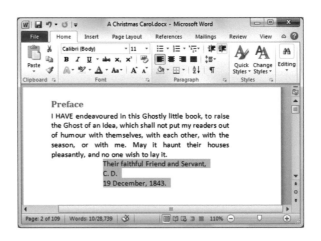

4 Adjust the formatting and alignment of the text, as desired, for example selecting Justify for the main portion and Increase Indent for the signature section

5 Select Save, on the Quick Access toolbar

Update Table of Contents

When you make changes, such as to the preface or the illustrations list, that include new headings (level 1, 2 or 3), the table of contents is affected. However, the updates will not be displayed immediately. To apply the updates:

1 Locate the table of contents and click anywhere within it

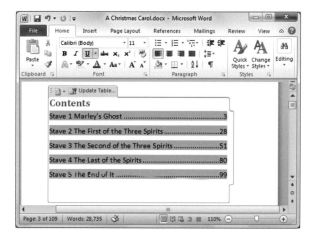

59

2 Select Update entire table to add new items, and click OK

3 The new entries will be inserted, and all the page numbers will be updated, as appropriate

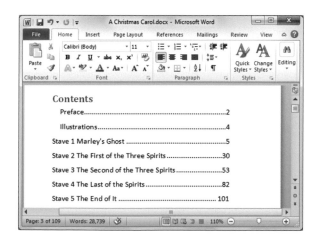

Hot tip

Whenever you add text to the document, or insert pages, the page numbers for the entries in the table of contents change, but the changes will not appear until you explicitly select Update Table.

Don't forget

If you've added pages or text to your document, but have not changed the headings, select Update page numbers only.

Decorate the Page

1 Select sections of text and choose the appropriate format

Finally, you can enhance the formatting of the title page, using styles or WordArt.

2 For example, select the book title and choose the Title style. There are also Subtitle and various Emphasis styles

Title style

Subtitle style

Intense Emphasis

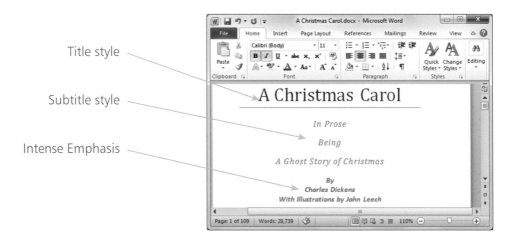

3 For more impact, select the item of text and, from the Insert tab, choose the WordArt option in the text group

4 Review the WordArt styles offered and select an option

Hot tip

The WordArt effects are not displayed during Insert until you select a specific option. You can select a different option, or clear the WordArt if you change your mind.

5 The text is displayed in the selected style and color

6 Explore the WordArt Styles, and the Text Fill, Outline, and Effects options

Don't forget

This illustrates the Glow and Double Wave, two of the transforms offered in the Text Effects.

Templates

1 Click the File tab, select New, and choose a Sample template, or select one of your installed templates

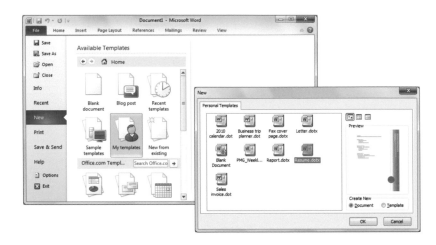

2 For a new requirement, select the relevant Office Online category (and subcategory if offered), or carry out a search to find the most suitable template for your purpose

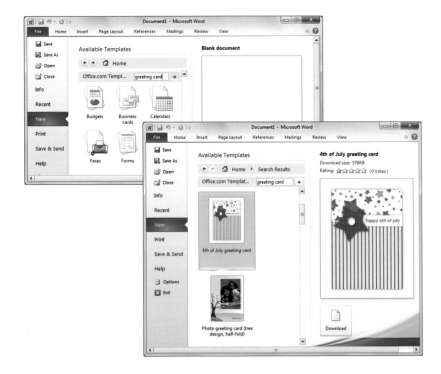

3 Click the Download button for the template, and the file will be copied to your hard disk

4 When the transfer completes, a new document is opened using the chosen template

Hot tip

When you download a template, it is added to My Templates (and to Recent Templates), so that you won't have to download it the next time it's needed.

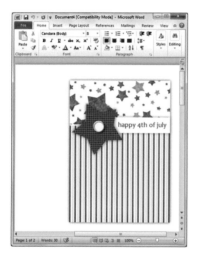

5 Change the contents of the text box to personalize the document, or delete the text for a handwritten message

6 In future, you can select New, My Templates to use the template to create another document of that type

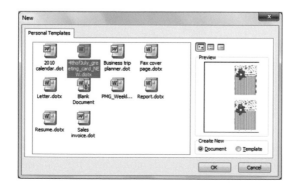

Don't forget

This template is a two fold document that contains two copies of the greetings card

Publisher

Publisher provides a higher level of desktop publishing capability, with a great variety of paper sizes and styles, including many templates for brochures and leaflets, etc., and lots of guidance.

1 Start the Publisher application, which opens in BackStage view, and select a category, such as Greeting Cards

2 Open the subcategory All Occasions and Events, and explore the templates offered

3 Click any template in the group to see an enlarged version, and details of the color and font schemes

Create a Publication

1 Choose a template, such as Congratulations 2, then click the Create button

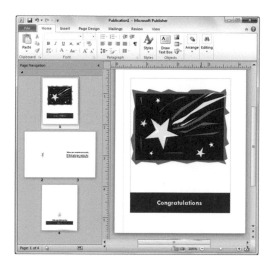

Don't forget

The greeting card is divided into four sections, each one-quarter of the physical page, making it easier to view and edit individual parts of the card.

2 Click section 2 & 3 to see the middle portion of the card

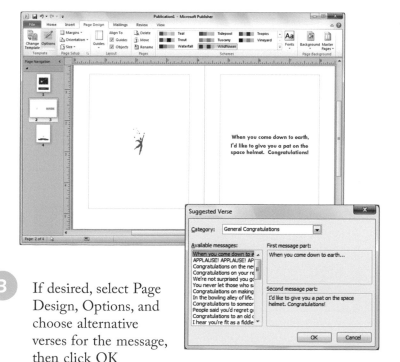

Hot tip

You can make changes to the suggested verses, before you click OK, or at any time afterwards.

3 If desired, select Page Design, Options, and choose alternative verses for the message, then click OK

Print the Publication

1 Click section 4 to see the back portion of the card

Publisher presents the card in a professional format, complete with maker's attribution. You can edit this text before printing the document.

2 Select File, Print, to see the document as it appears on paper – a single sheet, with sections 2 and 3 inverted

Once printed, the page is folded in half, horizontally, then in half again, to form the greeting card.

3 Adjust the settings as required, then click the Print button

4 Calculations

This looks at Excel, the spreadsheet application, and covers creating a new workbook, entering data, replicating values, formatting numbers, adding formulas and functions, and using templates.

Start Excel

To start Microsoft Excel with a fresh new spreadsheet, with temporary name Book1:

1 Click Start, All Programs, Microsoft Office and Microsoft Office Excel 2010, to open with Book1

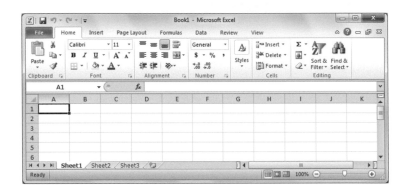

2 Alternatively, right-click an empty part of a folder window; select New, Microsoft Office Excel Worksheet

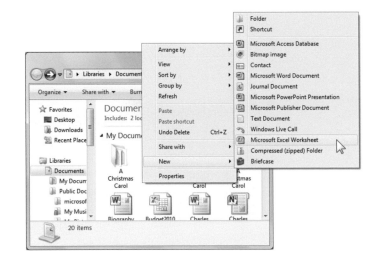

3 Double-click the file icon New Microsoft Office Excel Worksheet, to display and edit the document

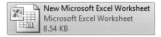

The spreadsheet presented is an Excel workbook that contains, initially, three worksheets, each of which is blank. The cells that it contains are empty – all 17 million of them.

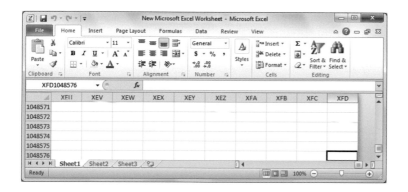

Hot tip

There can be up to 1048576 rows and 16384 columns. Compared with 65536 rows and 256 columns in previous releases.

1 To move to the last row (1048576) in the worksheet, press End, and then press the down arrow

2 To move to the last column (XFD) in the worksheet, press End, and then press the right arrow

If the worksheet contains data, the action taken depends on the initial location.

Beware

It may be impractical to utilize even a fraction of the total number of cells available, but the enlarged sheet size does give greater flexibility in designing spreadsheets. For larger amounts of data, you should use Access (see page 104).

3 If the selected cell contains data, pressing End and then an arrow key takes you to the edge of the data area

4 If the current cell is empty, you move to the start of the adjacent data area

5 If there's no more data in that direction, you'll move to the edge of the worksheet, as with an empty worksheet

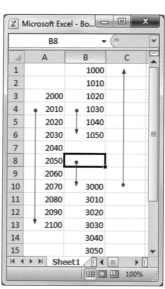

Don't forget

The movement is always in the direction of the arrow key selected.

69

Enter Data

The most common use of spreadsheets is for financial planning, for example to keep track of income and expenditure. To create a family budget:

Hot tip

You can find ready-made, budget spreadsheets and templates at the Microsoft Office website, and on other Internet locations. However, it is useful to create such a spreadsheet from scratch, to illustrate the processes involved.

1 Open a blank worksheet, select cell A1 and type the title for the spreadsheet, e.g. Family Budget

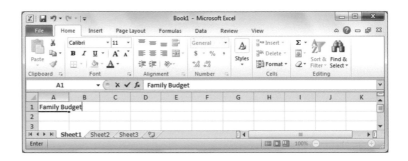

2 Press the Enter or down key to insert the text and move to cell A2, then type the next entry, Income

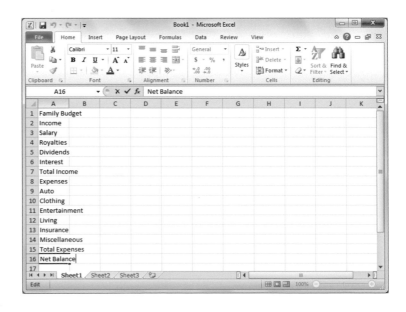

Don't forget
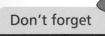

You can change the format of the labels to highlight entries, such as Title, Income, and Expenses (see page 76).

3 Repeat this process to add the remaining labels for the income and expense items you want to track, and labels for the totals and balance

If you omit an item, you can insert an additional worksheet row. For example, to include a second Salary income item:

1 Click a cell (e.g. C4) in the row that's just below where the new entry is required, and select Insert, Insert Sheet Rows from the Cells group on the Home tab

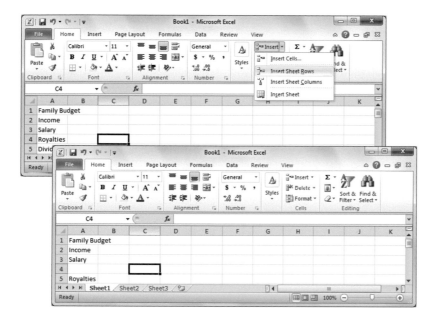

71

2 Enter the additional label, e.g. "Salary 2nd", in A4

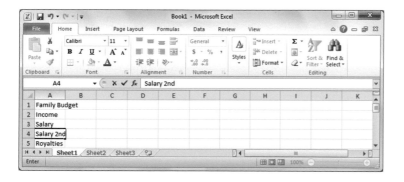

Don't forget

You can also select the cell and press F2, or click anywhere on the formula bar, to make changes to the content of a cell.

2	Income
3	Salary 1st
4	Salary 2nd

3 Double-click an existing cell to edit or retype the entry, to change "Salary" to "Salary 1st" in A3 for example

Quick Fill

You can create one column of data, then let Excel replicate the cell contents for you. For example:

1 Enter month and values in column C, January in C2 and values in cells C3–C7 and C10–C15 for example

Don't forget

You can widen column A to accommodate the whole text (see page 78), then delete column B.

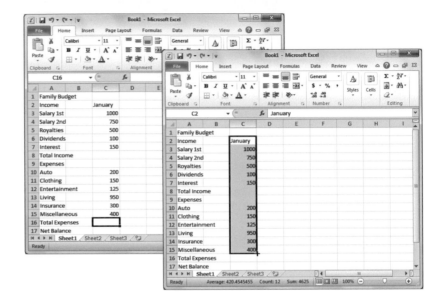

Hot tip

Click in cell C2, hold down the Shift key and click in cell C15 to highlight the whole range of cells.

2 Highlight cells C2–C15, move the mouse pointer over the box at the bottom right, and, when it becomes a **+,** drag it to the right to replicate the cells for further months

72

3 Release the mouse pointer when the required number of columns is indicated

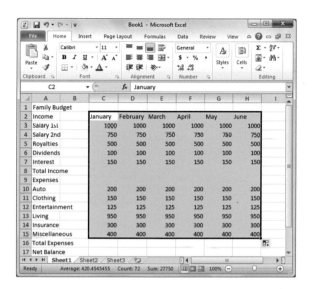

Hot tip

Excel detects weekdays to create a series, such as Monday, Tuesday ...; and it detects abbreviated names, such as Jan, Feb ... or Mon, Tue ....

Don't forget

Having initialized the cells, you can edit or replace the contents of individual cells to finalize the data.

73

4 Numeric values are duplicated, but the month name is detected and the succeeding months are inserted

After you've used the Fill handle, the Auto Fill Options button appears. Click this to control the action, for example to replicate the formatting only, or to copy cells without devising a series.

5 As you enter data into the worksheet, remember to periodically click the Save button on the Quick Access toolbar

Don't forget

The first time you click the Save button, you'll be prompted to provide a file name in place of the default Book1.

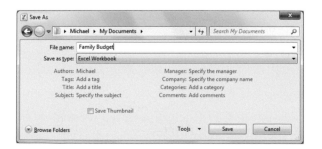

Sums and Differences

When you've entered the data, and made the changes required, you can introduce functions and formulas to complete the worksheet.

1 Click cell C8 (total income for January), then select the Home tab and click the Sum button

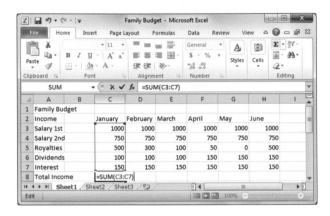

2 Press Enter to show the total, then repeat the procedure for cell C16 (total expenses for January)

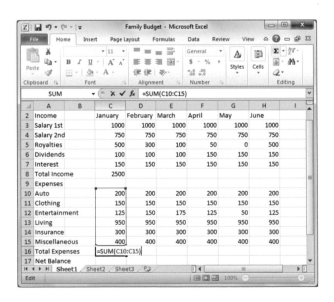

3 Click in cell C17 (the cell reserved for the net balance for the month of January)

4 Type =, click C8, type -, and then click C16 (to calculate total income for January minus total expenses for January)

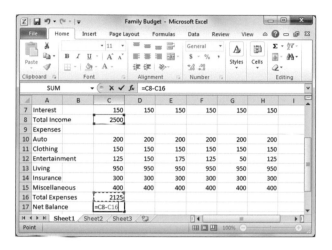

Hot tip

The = symbol indicates that the following text is a formula. You can type the cell references, or click on the cell itself, and Excel will enter the appropriate reference.

75

5 Press Enter to complete the formula and display the result

6 Select cell C8 and use the Fill handle to replicate the formula for the other months (e.g. February to June), and repeat this process for cells C16 and C17

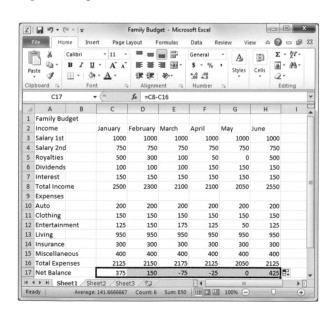

Don't forget

When the formula is replicated, the cell references, e.g. C8:C16, are incremented, to D8:D16, E8:E16 etc.

Formatting

Hot tip

Changing the format for various parts of the worksheet can make it easier to review and assess the results.

1 Click A1 (the title cell), then select the Home tab, choose a larger font size, and select a font effect, such as Bold

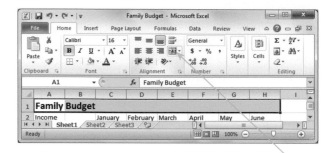

2 Press Shift, and click H1 to highlight the row across the data, then click the Merge and Center button

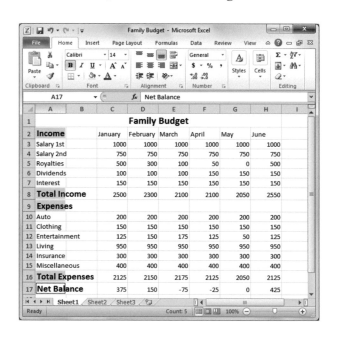

Don't forget

You can change each cell individually, or press Ctrl and click each of the cells to select them, then apply the changes to all the cells at once.

3 Click the Categories and Totals labels (e.g. A2, A8, A9, A16, A17), and change the font size and effects

4 Alternatively, click Styles to pick a suitable cell style

To emphasize the "Net Balance" values for each month:

1 Select the range of cells, e.g. C17:H17

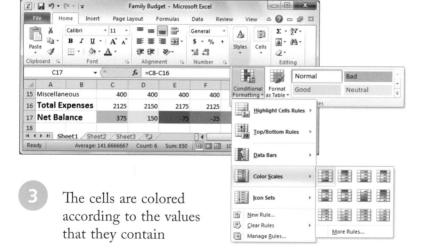

Excel 2010 includes a very useful Conditional Formatting facility, where the effects applied depend on the actual contents of the cells being formatted.

2 Select Styles, Conditional Formatting, Color Scales and choose for example the Green–Yellow–Red color scale

3 The cells are colored according to the values that they contain

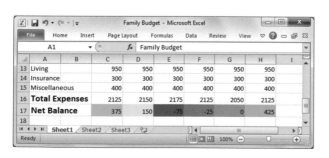

Don't forget

Positive balances are green; the larger the balance, the deeper the shade. Modest balances are yellow; while shades of red are applied to negative balances.

Rounding Up

You can use Excel functions, such as Round Up or Ceiling, to adjust the solutions of numerical problems, such as the number of tiles needed to cover the floor area of a room.

1 Open a new, blank worksheet, and enter these labels in the first column:

Number of Tiles
Tile Length
Tile Width
Room Length
Room Width
Number of Tiles
Per Box
Boxes

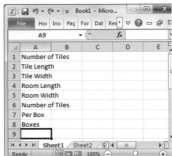

2 Enter sample sizes in cells B2:B5, making sure that you use the same units for the tile and room dimensions

3 In cell B6, type the formula =(B4/B2)*(B5/B3)

4 In cell B8, type the formula =B6/B7

For these figures, and on the basis of these calculations, you might think 5 boxes would be sufficient. However, if you fit the tiles to the area, you find that some tiles have to be trimmed. The wastage leaves part of the area uncovered.

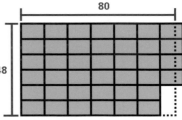

To ensure that there are enough whole tiles to completely cover the area, you need to round up the evaluations:

1 Copy B2:B8 to C2:C8, and, in cell C6, type the formula =CEILING(B4/B2,1)*CEILING(B5/B3,1)

Hot tip

The CEILING function rounds the results up to the next significant value, in this case, the next highest integer. If the tiles have a repeat pattern, you might need to use the pattern size as the significant number.

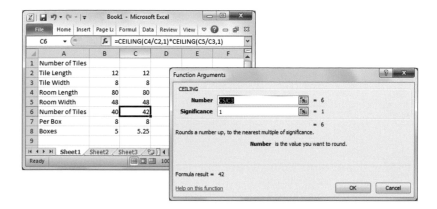

The number of whole tiles increases to 42, which will now cover the complete floor area, even after cutting.

This gives 5.25 boxes. Assuming that boxes must be purchased in whole numbers, this result also needs rounding up.

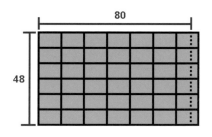

Don't forget

The ROUNDUP function is another way to adjust values. Here it is used to round up the result to zero decimal places, which also gives the next highest integer.

2 Copy C2:C8 to D2:D8, and, in cell D8, type the formula =ROUNDUP(D6/D7,0) to get the result: 6 boxes

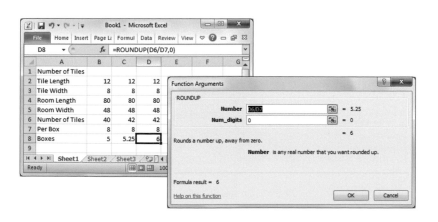

Find a Function

There are a large number of functions available in Excel, they are organized into a library of groups to make it easier to find the one you need.

1 Select the Formulas tab to show the Function Library

2 Click a category in the Function Library, for an alphabetic list of functions it offers

3 If you don't know where to search for the function you want, click the Insert Function button

4 Choose a category, and pick a function from the list

5 Alternatively, type a description and click Go, then select one of the recommended functions

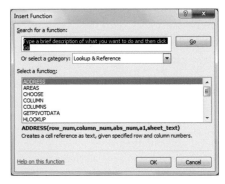

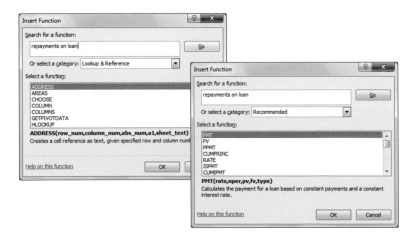

6 Select a suitable function, e.g. PMT, and click OK

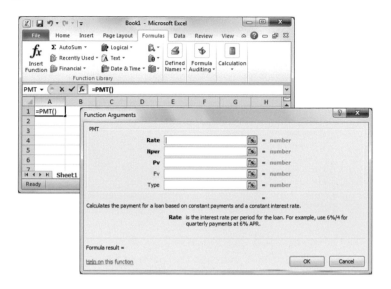

7 Type the values for the arguments (Rate, Nper, etc.), using the description provided as you select each item

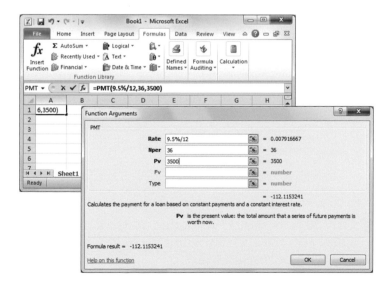

8 The result is displayed (a negative figure, indicating a payment) and the function is inserted into the worksheet

Goal Seeking

Using the PMT function, you can establish the monthly payments required to pay off a long-term loan over, say, 25 years.

Hot tip

To calculate payments for an interest-only loan, set Fv (see page 81) to the same value as the loan amount.

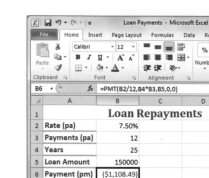

Suppose, however, you'd like to know how many years it will take to pay off the loan if you increase the payments to, say, $1500.

1 One way to establish this is by trial and error, adjusting the number of years until you get the required payment

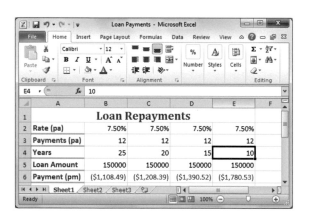

Don't forget

You would carry on refining your estimate, e.g. trying 12 then 14, to discover that the correct answer lies between these two periods.

2 Try 20 years, then 15 years, then 10 years, the payment then goes above $1500. So the appropriate period would be between 10 and 15 years

However, Excel provides an automatic way to apply this type of process, and this can give you an exact answer very quickly.

1 Click the cell containing the function, select the Data tab, and click the What If Analysis button in Data Tools

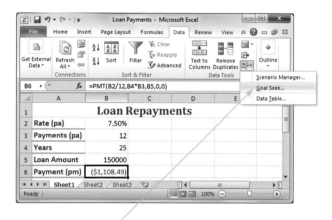

Hot tip

Use the Scenario Manager to create a set of results for a range of values, such as 10, 15 and 20 years of repayments.

2 Select the Goal Seek option and specify the required result −1500 (payment per month) and the change to cell B4 (number of years)

3 Goal Seeking tries out various values for the changing cell, until the desired solution is found

Beware

You must specify the target payment as a negative value, since it is a repayment, otherwise Goal Seeking will be unable to find a solution.

4 Click OK to see the revised results displayed in the worksheet

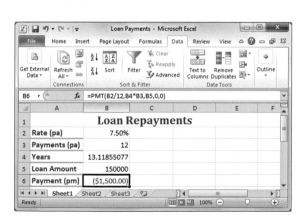

Templates

1 Select the File tab and click the New button

2 Select Installed Templates, or "My Templates", to choose from the list of templates already on your system

3 Select a category to review the templates from Microsoft Office Online, choose a template, and then click Download to install it on your system

5 Manage Data

Excel also manages data, so we will look at importing data, applying sorts and filters, and selecting specific sets of data. The data can be used to create a chart, or you can arrange the data in tables, insert totals and computations, and look up values. Some editions of Office include Access, which offers full database management functions.

Import Data

You don't always need to type in all the information in your worksheets, if the data is already available in another application. For example, to import data from a delimited text file:

Hot tip

Excel can retrieve data from any application that can create files in a delimited text file format, such as CSV (comma-separated values), or from database systems, such as SQL Server, Access, dBase, FoxPro, Oracle, and Paradox.

Don't forget

Identify the appropriate file type to select from, in this case, Text Files.

1 Click the File tab and select Open

2 Select the file that contains the data you wish to import and click Open to start the Text Import Wizard, which recognizes the delimited file. Click Next to continue

3 Choose the delimiter (e.g. Comma) and click Next

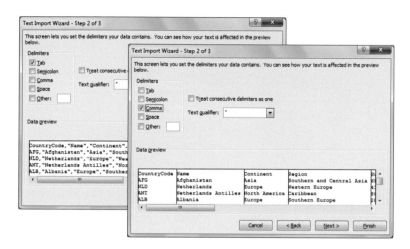

4 Adjust column formats, if required, then click Finish

5 The data is presented in the form of an Excel worksheet

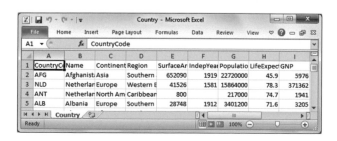

Explore the Data

Don't forget

Select the File tab, click Save As and choose file type Excel Workbook, to save the data as a standard Excel file.

 Save As

① Double-click or drag the separators between the columns to reveal more of the data they contain

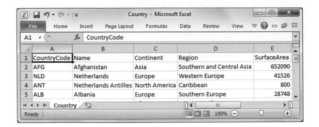

② Select the View tab, click Freeze Panes in the Window group, and select Freeze Top Row

 Hot tip

Freezing the top row makes the headings it contains visible, whichever part of the worksheet is being displayed.

③ Press Ctrl+End to move to the last cell in the data area

 Hot tip

This will show you how many rows and columns there are in the data (in this example, 240 rows and 13 columns).

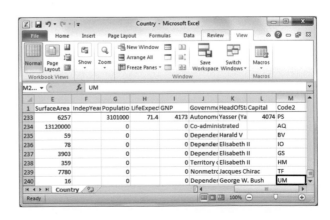

Sort

1 Click a cell in the Name column, select the Data tab and click the A–Z (ascending) button to sort by name

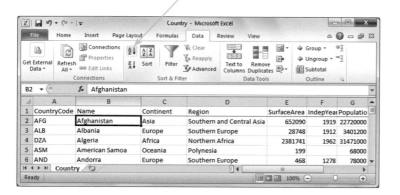

Don't forget

You can also select the Sort options from within the Editing group on the Home tab.

2 Click a cell in the Population column and click the Z–A (sort descending) button, to sort from highest to lowest

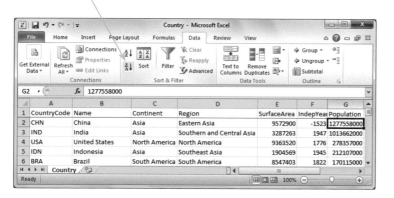

Hot tip

If you click in a single cell, Excel will select all the surrounding data and sort whole rows into the required order.

3 To sort by more than one value, click the Sort button

Don't forget

You can sort the data into sequence using several levels of values.

...cont'd

Beware

If a selection of the worksheet is highlighted when you click one of the buttons, the sort may be restricted to the selected data.

Don't forget

For data organized by columns, rather than rows, click the Options button and select Sort left to right.

4 Click the arrow in the Sort by box and select the main sort value, for example, Continent

5 Click the Add Level button and select the additional sort values, for example, Region and then Population

6 Change the sort sequence, if needed, then click OK to sort the data by population within region and continent

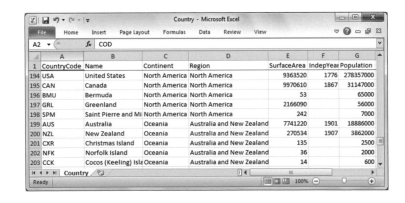

Filters

You can filter the data to hide entries that are not of immediate interest.

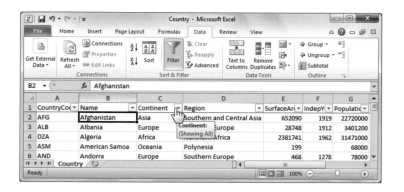

1. Click a cell within the data area, select the Data tab and click the Filter button in the Sort & Filter group

2. Click a filter icon, e.g. Continent, to display its AutoFilter

3. Click the Select All box, to deselect all entries, then select the specific entry you want, e.g. Oceania

4. Click OK to apply the filter

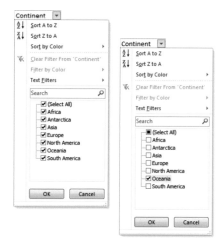

Hot tip

You can also select the Filter button from within the Editing group on the Home tab (see page 89).

Hot tip

Filtering is turned on, and a filter icon (an arrow) is added to each heading, with an initial setting of Showing All.

Number Filters

Don't forget

You can set number filters, where you specify a level at which to accept or reject entries, or choose an option, such as accepting the top ten entries.

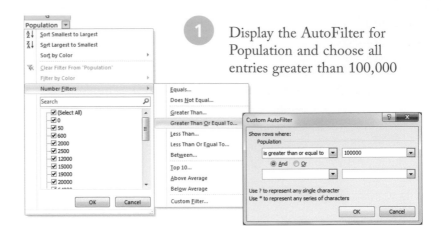

1 Display the AutoFilter for Population and choose all entries greater than 100,000

2 The filter icons for modified AutoFilters are changed, to show that filtering is in effect for those particular columns

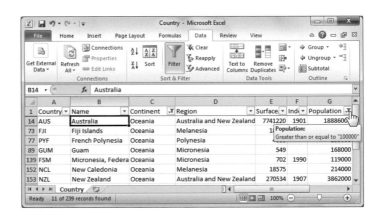

Beware

If you click the Filter button on the Data tab, or the Home tab, it will remove all the filters and delete all the filter settings.

Filter

3 Click a filter icon and select the Clear Filter option, to remove the filter for a particular column

4 The filter icon for that column reverts to an arrow, and the Showing All option will be applied

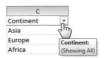

Select Specific Data

Suppose you want to examine the population values for the larger countries. You can hide away information that's not relevant for that purpose:

1. Use the AutoFilter on the Population column, to display only countries whose populations are greater than 150 million

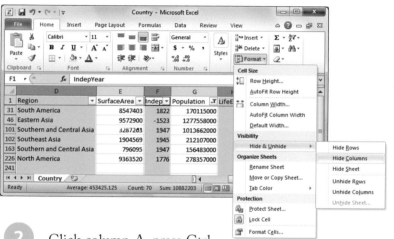

2. Click column A, press Ctrl, click columns C, D etc. and select Home, Format, Hide & Unhide, Hide Columns

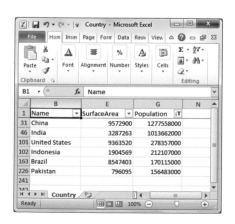

This places the column of country names adjacent to the columns of surface area and population values, ready for further analysis, creating a chart for example.

3. The display will be restricted to the required data

Create a Chart

1 Highlight the data (including headers), then select the Insert tab and click the arrow on the Charts group

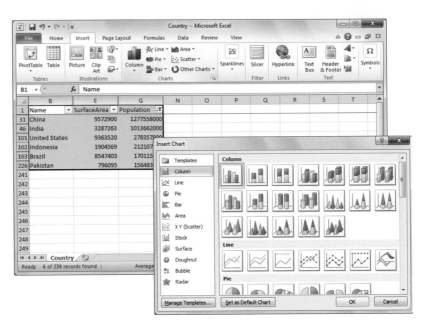

2 Choose the chart type and subtype, in this case, Column and Clustered Column

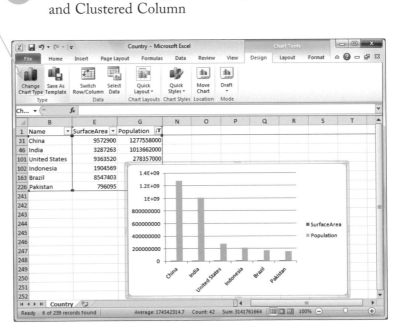

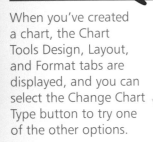

3 Click one of the Population columns and select Format Data Series

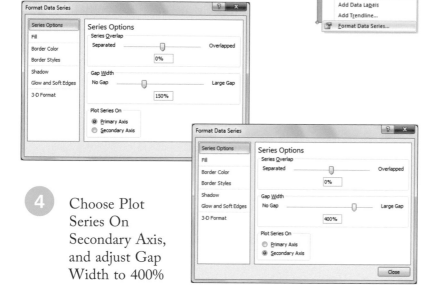

4 Choose Plot Series On Secondary Axis, and adjust Gap Width to 400%

By default, one data series would overlay the other, but adjusting the width for one of them allows you to view both sets of data together.

5 Use the Layout tab to provide titles for the chart and the axes, and to adjust the position of the legend

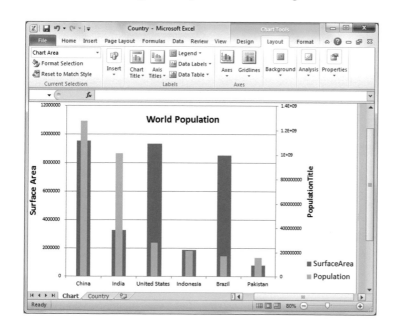

Don't forget

Select the Move Chart button on the Design tab to place the chart on a separate worksheet.

Import a List

The Country worksheet used as an example includes the Capital column, which provides a link to a list of cities. This list is available as a text file, so it can be imported into the worksheet.

1 Select a cell marking the start of an empty section of the worksheet, and then click the Data tab

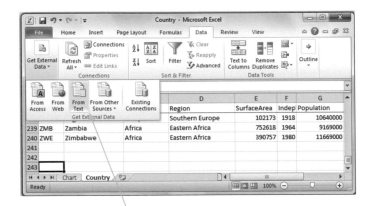

2 Click Get External Data and choose From Text

City
Text Document
183 KB

3 Locate the text file, click Import, then follow the steps in the Text Import Wizard (see page 86)

4 Click OK to place the data in the current worksheet, at the location selected initially

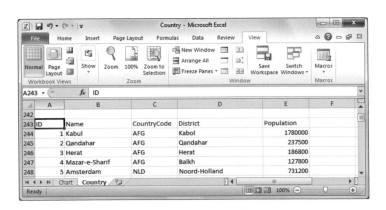

Create a Table

1 Click a cell within the data range and select the Insert tab, then click the Table button

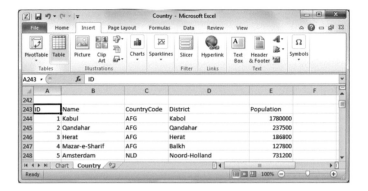

Hot tip

To make it easier to manage and analyze the data in the list, you can turn the range of cells into an Excel table.

2 Click Yes to confirm the range and accept the headers

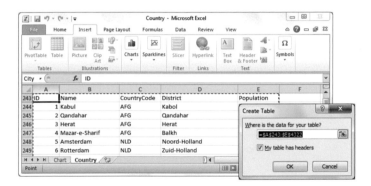

Don't forget

When you create a table from a data range, any connection with the external data source will be removed.

3 The table will be created (using the default style)

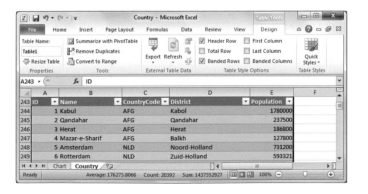

Hot tip

Change the default name (Table1 or similar) to something that's more relevant to the content, such as City.

Add Totals to Table

1 Click a cell within the country data and select Insert, Table, then rename the new table as Country

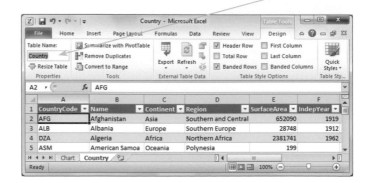

2 Select the Table Tools Design tab, then click the box for the Total Row, which is displayed at the end of the table

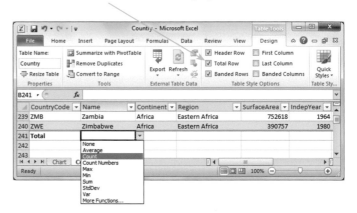

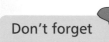

3 Select the Total box for Name, click the arrow and choose the appropriate function, e.g. Count

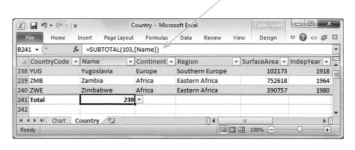

4 Select the Sum function for columns with numerical values, such as SurfaceArea, Population, or GNP

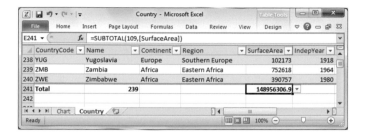

Hot tip

You do not use the column and row labels to specify cells and ranges, you use the header name for the column (enclosed in square brackets).

5 You can combine functions, such as Min and Max, to show the range of values in a column, e.g. IndepYear

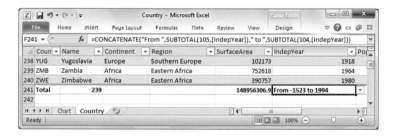

Don't forget

You can use any Excel function in the total boxes, not just the set of subfunctions in Subtotal.

6 When a column contains a set of discrete values, such as Continent or Region, you can calculate the number of unique values it contains

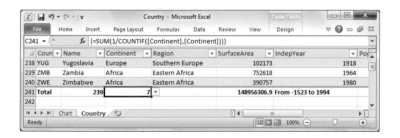

Hot tip

You can type an array formula without the enclosing curly braces { }, then press Ctrl+Shift+Enter, instead of the usual Enter, and the braces are added automatically.

This is an array formula that counts the number of times each particular value in the column is repeated, and uses these repeats to build up a count of the number of distinct values.

Computed Column

You can insert a column in the table without affecting other ranges, data or tables in the worksheet.

1 Click in the Population column, select the Home tab, click Insert, and choose Insert Table Columns to the Left

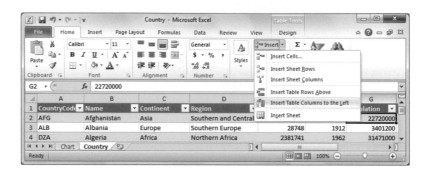

2 The new column is inserted and initially named Column1

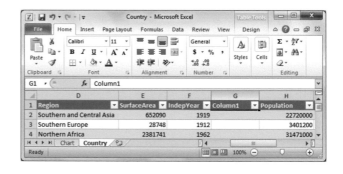

3 Type a new name, such as Density, and press Enter

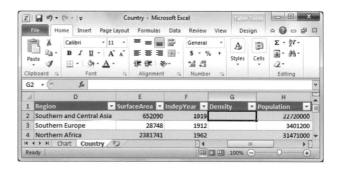

4   Click in the first cell of the column, and type =, then click the Population cell in the same row

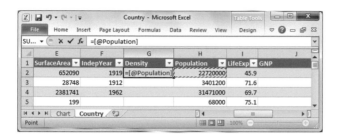

Hot tip

The cell that you select is referenced as the current row of Population, in the form: [@Population].

5   Type /, then click the SurfaceArea cell in the same row

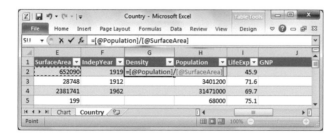

Hot tip

The next cell you select is referenced as: [@SurfaceArea]

6   Press Enter, the expression is evaluated and copied to all the other cells in the table column

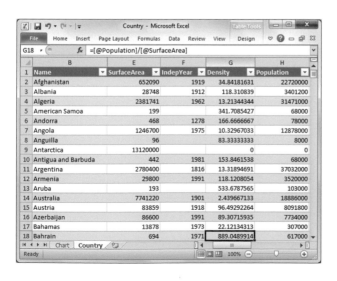

Don't forget

The result is the population density, the number of people per square kilometer. You can format the values in the cells, if desired.

G	
Density	▼
	34.84
	118.31
	13.21

Don't forget

The formula in each cell refers to [@ColName], which is the current row for the named column.

Table Lookup

The Country table contains a city code number for the capital city of each country, rather than the actual name.

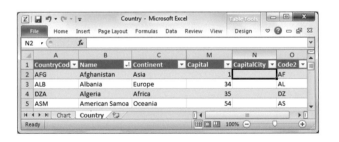

The names are stored in the separate City table, which has details of more than 4000 cities.

To display the name of the capital city alongside the city number, in the Country table:

1 Insert a table column next to the Capital column and change its name to CapitalCity

2 Click the first cell of the new column and type the expression =VLOOKUP(

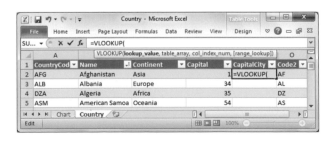

③ Click the adjacent cell in the Capital column, then type the expression ,City,2,0)

④ Press Enter, and the capital city name is inserted on all the rows in the Country table, not just the current row

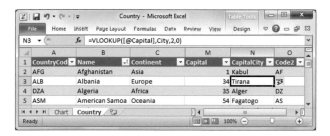

⑤ Scroll down to check the entries for particular countries, the United States (Washington) or the United Kingdom (London) for example

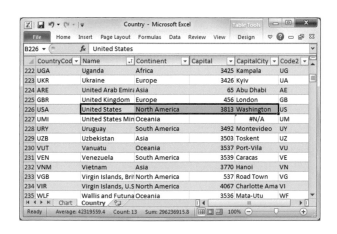

Manage Data Using Access

Hot tip

You'll find Access 2010 in the Professional editions of Office 2010.

If you have large amounts of data, or complex functions to handle, you may require the more comprehensive facilities in Access 2010.

1 Start Access from the Office folder on the Start menu and you'll be greeted by a range of database templates

Don't forget

Access uses the Office 2010 Fluent user interface (Ribbon technology), and can share data with other Office applications, such as Excel, Word, and PowerPoint.

2 Select a suitable template, for example, Assets, change the suggested name, if desired, and click the Download button

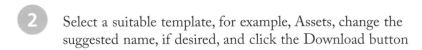

Hot tip

Access automatically displays a Help window, which offers advice on modifying and using your new database.

3 The template is downloaded and prepared for use, and a new database will be created

4 Select a user name and click Login, and the database opens

5 Click Enable Content to enable the VBA macros in the template

Don't forget

If there's no user defined, or if you want another user defined, click the New User button and provide the details

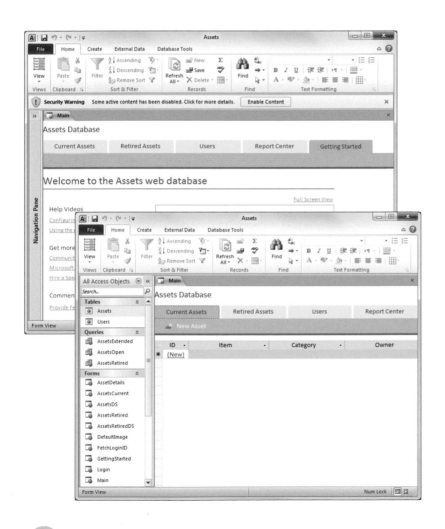

Beware

Do not enable macros in databases that you download, unless you are sure that the source of the file is trustworthy.

6 Click the Shutter Bar Open/Close button to display the database components (tables, queries, forms and reports), then click the Current Assets button

Add Records

1 Click the New Asset button to add an entry to the Current Assets database

2 Enter the details for the item, selecting from a list of values on fields with an arrow, e.g. Category

3 If the value you want is not listed, just right-click the box and select Edit List Items

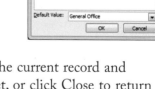

4 Add or change entries as required, and click OK

5 Click Save then New, to save the current record and begin the record for a new asset, or click Close to return to the list

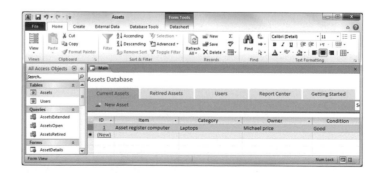

6 Presentations

Build a presentation, slide by slide, apply themes to create a consistent effect, and use animation to focus attention on particular points. Use a second monitor for a presenter view. Take advantage of templates, built in or downloaded, and print handouts for the presentation. Rehearse the show, to get timings, and create an automatic show.

Start a Presentation

Like all the Office 2010 applications, PowerPoint uses the Ribbon interface, which displays tabs appropriate to the current activity.

To start PowerPoint and create a presentation:

1 Select Start, All Programs, Microsoft Office, and click the PowerPoint entry

Hot tip

When PowerPoint opens, it presents a single blank title slide, ready for you to begin a new presentation.

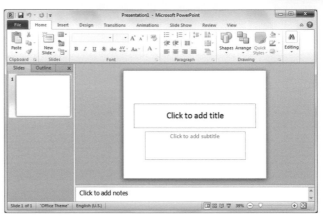

2 Click to add a title, as suggested, and type the title for the slide show, for example, Dickens World

Don't forget

By default, the presentation starts with a title slide, where two text boxes are predefined. If you don't want a particular text box, just ignore it – it won't appear on the slide unless you edit the text.

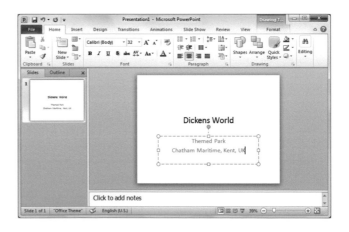

3 Click to add a subtitle, the second option, and type, e.g. Themed Park, Chatham Maritime, Kent, UK (the childhood home of Charles Dickens)

4 Select the Home tab and click the New Slide button in the Slides group

5 A new slide, with text boxes for title and content, will be added to the slide show

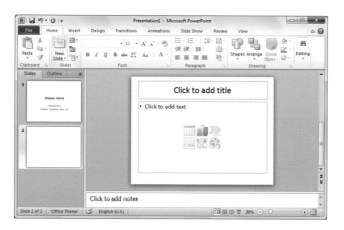

Hot tip

The new slide has option buttons to insert a table, chart, SmartArt graphic, or picture from a file, clip art or media clip. See page 111 for an example.

109

6 Click on the prompts and add the title Features of Dickens World, then type bullet points to give the details

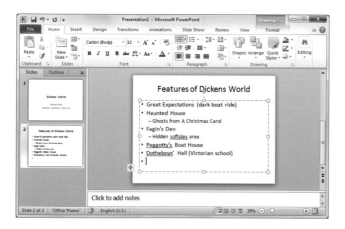

7 Press Enter to add a new bullet item, and then press the Tab key to move to the next lower level of bullet items

Don't forget

Click within a bullet item and press Shift+Tab to move it up (promote it) to the next level.

Expand the Slide

1 Click the button to Save your presentation

2 Continue to add items, you'll see the text size and spacing adjusted to fit the text onto the slide

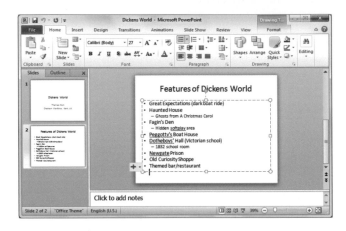

Don't forget

Alternatively, you can choose to stop fitting text to the placeholder, to continue on a new slide, or to change to a two-column format.

110

3 Click the AutoFit Options button that appears when the slide is filled, and select the option to Split Text Between Two Slides

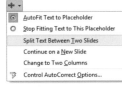

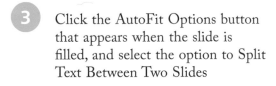

Hot tip

The text size and spacing will be re-adjusted to take advantage of the extra space available.

4 A new slide is inserted, with the same layout and title as the original slide, and the bullet items are shared evenly between the two slides

Insert a Picture

1 Select the Home tab, then click the arrow on the New Slide button in the Slides group to display the options

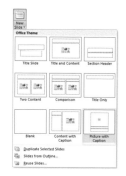

2 Choose a slide layout, such as Picture with Caption

3 Click the icon to add a picture, as suggested in the prompt

Hot tip

There are nine standard layouts for slides, so you can select the one that's most appropriate for the specific content planned for each slide.

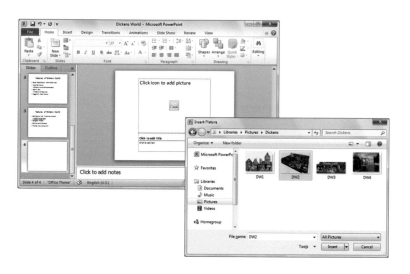

4 Locate and select the image file and click Insert, then select in turn Click to add title, and Click to add text

Don't forget

The title and the text you add provide the caption for the inserted image.

Apply a Theme

The default slides have a plain background, but you can choose a more effective theme, and apply it to all the slides you've created.

Hot tip

The selected theme is temporarily applied to the current slide, to help you choose the most effective theme.

1 Select the Design tab, and move the mouse pointer over each of the themes, to see the effect

Beware

To avoid losing your results, make sure you save the presentation periodically. Click the Save icon on the Quick Access toolbar, or press the Ctrl+S shortcut key.

2 Click the preferred theme to apply it to all of the slides in the presentation

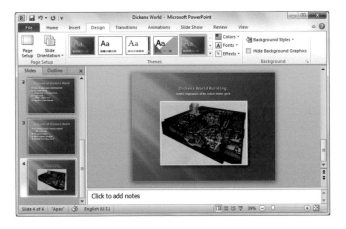

Don't forget

You can right-click your selected theme and choose to apply it to selected slides, or set the theme as the default for future slides.

Apply to All Slides
Apply to Selected Slides
Set as Default Theme
Add Gallery to Quick Access Toolbar

3 You can scroll the list to display additional themes, change the colors, fonts, and effects for the current theme, and modify the type of background style it uses

To select the transition effects between slides:

1 Select the Transitions tab and review the options – starting with None, Cut, Fade, Push

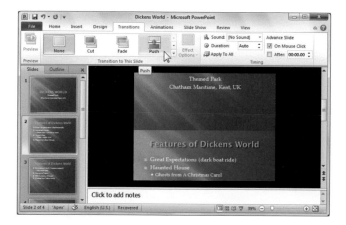

Hot tip

Move the mouse pointer over an effect to see it demonstrated on the current slide, e.g. Push from bottom.

2 Click the up and down arrows to view another of the 9 rows of effects

3 Click an effect to assign it to the current slide

Don't forget

When you have selected a transition, the Effects Options button is enabled, so you can choose variations of that transition.

By default, each slide advances to the next slide when you press the mouse key, but you can adjust the setting for individual slides.

4 Clear the On Mouse Click box to disable the mouse-key for the current slide

5 Select to Advance Slide After the specified time

6 Click the Apply To All button to apply the settings to all the slides in the presentation

Whatever the setting, you can always advance the slide show by pressing one of the keyboard shortcuts, such as N (next), Enter, Page Down, right arrow, or spacebar. To go back a step, you'd press P (previous), Page Up, left arrow, up arrow, or Backspace.

Don't forget

If you have specified animation effects for individual elements on a slide (see page 114), the Advance function invokes the next animation, rather than the next slide.

Animations

You can apply animation effects to individual parts of a slide.

1 Select the Animations tab, pick a slide with bullet items, and note that the Animate button is grayed (inactive)

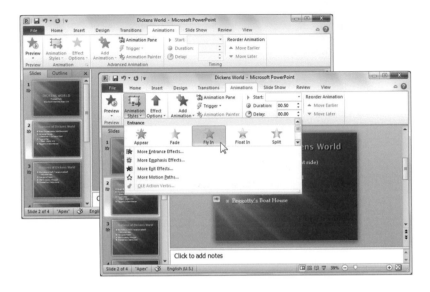

2 Select the text box with the bullet items, and the Animate button is activated

3 Click the down arrow on the Animate box and choose, for example, Fly In, By 1st Level Paragraph, then click the Preview button to observe the effect

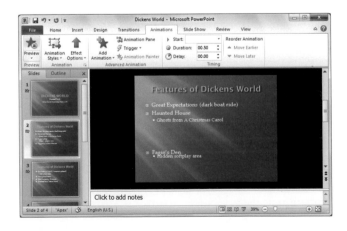

Run the Show

When you've added all the slides you need, you can try running the complete show, to see the overall effect.

1 Select the Slide Show tab and click the From the Beginning button in the Start Slide Show group

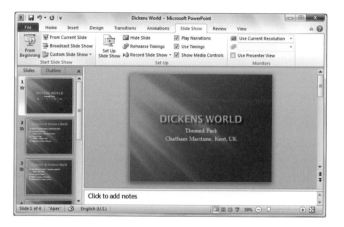

2 The slides are displayed full-screen, with the transition and animation effects that you selected

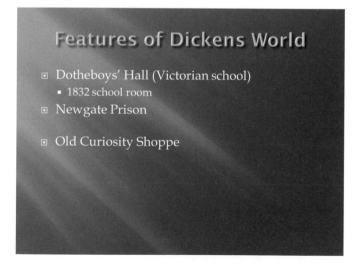

3 Click the mouse button to advance the slide show, animation by animation, or wait for the specified time period

115

Hot tip

You can also press F5 to run the slide show from the beginning, press Shift+F5 to run from the current slide, or press Esc to terminate.

Don't forget

You may need to use the mouse key, or the keyboard shortcuts, to go to the next slide or animation, if you haven't specified time limits for advancing slides.

Hot tip

When the slide show finishes, a black screen is presented, with the message: End of slide show, click to exit.

End of slide show, click to exit.

Other Views

116

Hot tip

This view is very helpful when you have a larger number of slides, since you can simply drag slides into their new positions.

Don't forget

Each slide and its notes will be displayed on a single sheet, which can be printed to make a very useful handout.

Hot tip

There's also a Reading View button, provided in the Presentation Views group on the Views tab, which allows you to view the slide show.

1 Select the View tab and select Slide Sorter to display all the slides, so that you can rearrange their sequence

2 Select the Notes Page view to see the current slide with its notes (information and prompts for the presenter)

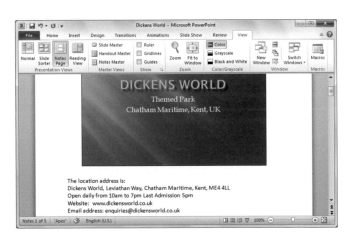

3 Click the Zoom button and select a zoom level, to examine parts of the slide or notes, then click OK

4 Select Fit and click OK (or click the Fit to Window button) to resize the view, to make the whole page visible

5 You can also drag the slider on the zoom bar to change the size

6 To switch back to the view with slide bar and current slide, click the Normal button

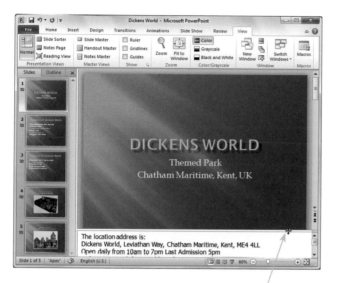

7 To reveal more of the notes area, click and drag the separator bar upwards

8 Click the Outline tab to see the text content of the slides, giving a summary view of the presentation

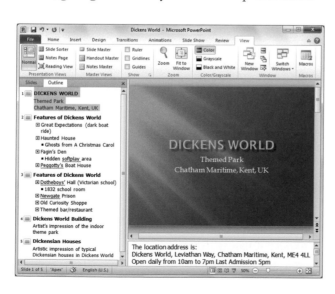

Presenter View

1 Select the Slide Show tab, and click the box to enable the Use Presenter View option

2 If you do not have a second monitor enabled, you'll be warned that this a requirement for Presenter View

3 Click Check, and the Display Settings panel is opened

4 Select the second monitor, and extend the desktop

5 Click Apply, then click Keep Changes when prompted, to enable the second monitor

6 With dual-monitor support enabled, you will be able to select the Use Presenter View option

7 Select the Slide Show tab and click the From Beginning button to present on two monitors

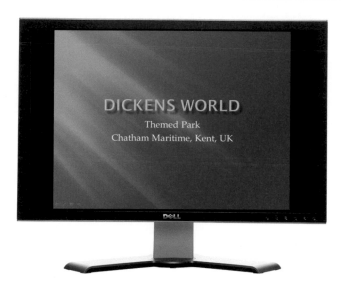

DICKENS WORLD
Themed Park
Chatham Maritime, Kent, UK

DICKENS WORLD
Themed Park
Chatham Maritime, Kent, UK

The location address is:
Dickens World, Leviathan Way,
Chatham Maritime, Kent, ME4 4LL
Open daily from 10am to 7pm
Last Admission 5pm
Website:
www.dickensworld.co.uk
Email address:
enquiries@dickensworld.co.uk

Slide: 1 of 5   Time: 00:03   9:39 PM   Zoom:

Use a Template

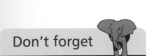

Hot tip

Templates provide ready-built presentations, which can be adapted to your needs. They also offer examples of useful PowerPoint techniques.

1 To review your templates, select the File tab, then click New, and select a category, e.g. Sample templates

2 Select a template, for example, Widescreen Presentation, and click the Create button to see the contents

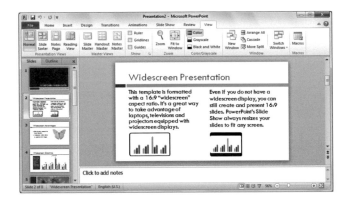

Don't forget

The templates that you open will be added to the Recent Templates list.

3 Select the View tab and Slide Sorter for an overview, or select the Slide Show tab to see the full presentation

4 Presentations you create from templates will be saved only when you explicitly select the Save command

Open one of the Photo Album templates:

1 Select the File tab, click New, Sample templates, then select Contemporary Photo Album and click Create

2 This displays sample pages to help you get started

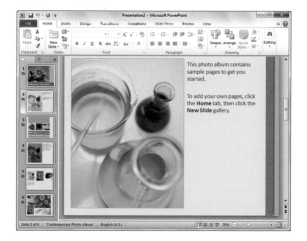

121

3 Select the Home tab and click New Slide, to review more than 20 different arrangements of photos and captions, choose the layout most suited to the pictures you want to display

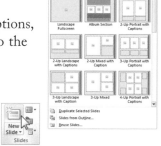

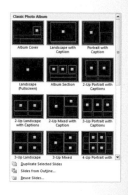

4 Click the New Slide button itself, to repeat the format of the current slide

Download a Template

1 Select the File tab, click New, and choose one of the Office.com Template categories

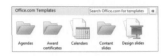

2 For example, Content Slides offers individual slides that can be downloaded and inserted into your presentations

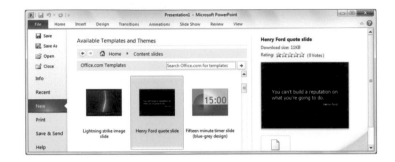

3 Select More templates, Name and place cards, then select the Numbered table tents template, and click the Download button

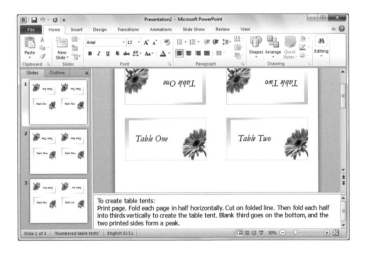

4 Follow the instructions in the notes, to print and prepare the table place tags, making changes to the text as needed

Print the Slide Show

1 Select the File tab, then click the Print button to specify the printer and other printing options

2 Select the printer you want to use, or accept the default printer

3 Enter slide numbers or ranges, and the Print All Slides setting changes to Custom Range

4 Click the Print Layout button to choose what type of document to print

5 You can print full page slides, slides with notes, or an outline

6 If you select Handouts, you can specify the number of slides to a page, and the order (horizontal or vertical)

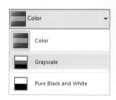

7 You can also select Frames Slides, Scale to Fit Paper, and High Quality printing

Rehearse Timings

To establish the timings for each slide, you need to rehearse the presentation and record the times for each step.

1 Select the Slide Show tab and click Rehearse Timings, which is in the Set Up group

2 The slide show runs full-screen in manual mode, with the timer superimposed in the top left corner

3 Advance each slide or animation, allowing for viewing and narration, etc. and the times will be recorded

4 When the presentation finishes, you can choose to keep the new slide timings for the next time you view the show

5 The view changes to Slide Sorter, with individual times for the slides. Make sure that Use Timings is selected

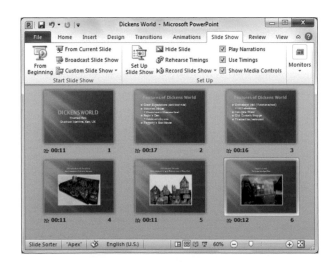

Save As Options

1 Select the File tab and the Info view is selected, with all the details of the presentation file

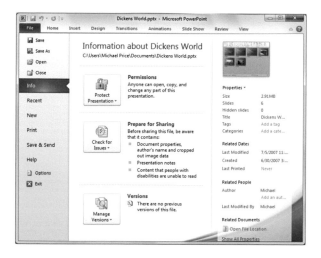

Hot tip

There are several forms you can save your PowerPoint 2010 Presentation in, including ways to share it with other users.

2 Click Save As, and then click the box labelled Save as type, to see what file formats are supported

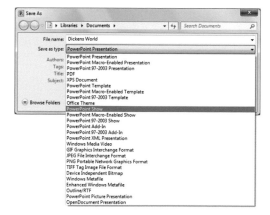

Don't forget

Save in the PowerPoint 97–2003 Show format (or Presentation format), to allow users with older versions of PowerPoint to view (or modify) the presentation.

3 PowerPoint Presentation (.pptx) is the default, and saves the presentation in a form that is suitable for editing

4 Select PowerPoint Show (.ppsx) for a form protected from modification, which opens in the Slide Show view

Package for CD

1 With the required presentation open, select the File tab, Save & Send, and then Package Presentation for CD

2 Type a name for the CD, add more presentations, if required, then click Copy to Folder

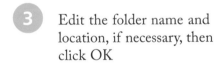

3 Edit the folder name and location, if necessary, then click OK

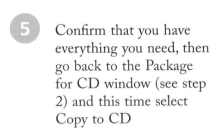

4 The presentation files are added to the folder, along with all the files needed to run the PowerPoint Viewer

5 Confirm that you have everything you need, then go back to the Package for CD window (see step 2) and this time select Copy to CD

6 You'll be prompted to insert a blank CD, and the files will then be added

7 Office Extras

OneNote is an extra
application that is on its way
to becoming mainstream.
There are more extras
included with all editions
of Office, including Picture
Manager, for editing
images, and Clip Organizer,
to manage media files.

OneNote 2010

The first version of OneNote 2003 was a stand-alone product. The next version, OneNote 2007, was incorporated in three of the Office 2007 editions. The latest version, OneNote 2010, is included in almost every edition of Office 2010 (see page 220) and is also one of the online Office Web Apps.

OneNote 2010 features Ribbon technology, supports the new BackStage view, and integrates with the other Office 2010 applications. There are also many new and improved features for search, editing, research, and note-taking, plus enhanced sharing and collaboration features.

All this suggests that OneNote may be ready to take its place as a fully–fledged member of the Microsoft Office family, alongside products like Word and Excel.

What is OneNote?

OneNote is the digital version of a pocket notebook, giving you the means to capture, organize, and access all of the information you need for a specific task or project, personal or collaborative, and in whatever the format of the data – typed, written, audio, video, figures, or photographs.

These are some of the things you can do:

- Color-code your OneNote notebook pages and sections
- Create, open, and search multiple notebooks at the same time
- Share notebooks with others, and take notes simultaneously
- Create OneNote side notes in other programs, so the notes are saved automatically in OneNote
- Insert screen captures from other application windows
- Send content from almost any program to OneNote
- Insert digital printouts of files, photos, audio, and videos
- Record audio or video from within OneNote
- Create Outlook tasks from OneNote, or insert Outlook calendar details into OneNote
- With a Tablet PC, make hand-written notes

Don't forget

The only place where you won't find OneNote is in the Starter Edition, which merely consists of subsets of Word and Excel.

Microsoft OneNote 2010

Hot tip

OneNote appends date and time stamps to screenshots, and includes the Web address and page titles automatically.

Hot tip

OneNote learns your handwriting, to make your written notes searchable, and converts them to text.

To start using OneNote 2010 on your computer:

1 Select Start, All Programs, Microsoft Office, and then Microsoft OneNote 2010

2 OneNote starts up and opens the Personal notebook, with the General section and the first of four pages selected

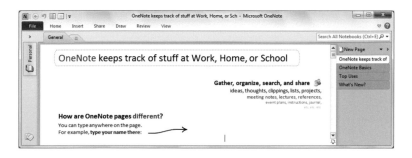

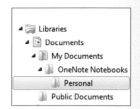

3 Scroll down the page to see how the Notebook, Section, and Page tabs relate to the parts of a paper notebook

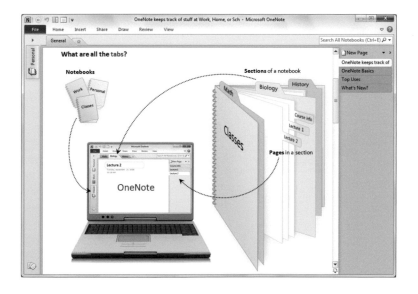

4 Scroll on to see some illustrations of typical OneNote notebooks, or select another page for more information

Create a Notebook

You can create a OneNote notebook from scratch:

1 Open OneNote and select the File tab, then click New

2 Choose where to place the notebook (Web, network, or your computer) and provide the name, e.g. Planning

Hot tip

The default location is the OneNote Notebooks, in the Documents folder for the active user name.

3 Edit the location, if necessary, then click Create Notebook

Don't forget

The OneNote Basics page in the guide gives some introductory advice for building your notebook.

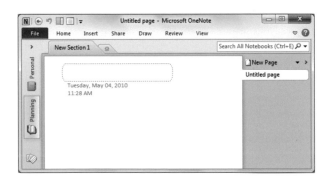

The notebook opens with a new section and an untitled page, ready for you to add notes, new pages, and new sections.

As with most Office applications, you will find it easier and more instructive to start from a suitable template.

1 Select the Help icon at the right (or press F1)

2 Select Getting started with OneNote 2010

3 Scroll down to the bottom of the page

4 Select the OneNote Notebooks link

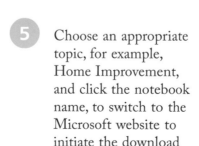

5 Choose an appropriate topic, for example, Home Improvement, and click the notebook name, to switch to the Microsoft website to initiate the download

Hot tip

See page 208 for more details of the online and offline help in Office.

Don't forget

There are also templates for pages that you can add to your notebook. Click the arrow next to New Page, and then select Page Templates.

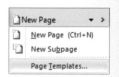

Download a Template

Don't forget

Select the hyperlink More in this category, to see a full list of the OneNote notebook templates available on the website.

1 At the website, click Download, for the required template

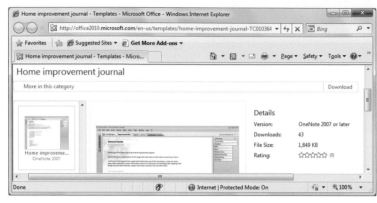

2 Downloading begins

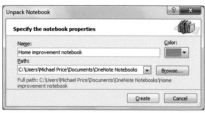

3 You are prompted to accept or amend the notebook name

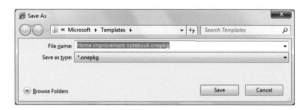

Hot tip

You may get a message saying that a Pop-up has been blocked. Click the message and select to allow pop-ups. It is usually best to make this a temporary option, for the current session only.

4 Click Create to confirm the save location, and unpack

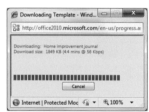

5 The notebook opens

Don't forget

The template may be based on an older version of OneNote, so would then open in compatibility mode.

To change the format of the new notebook:

1 Right-click the Notebook tab and select Properties

2 Click the button Convert to 2010

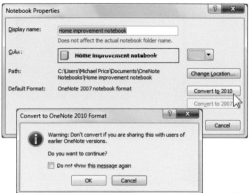

3 You are warned not to convert, if the notebook is shared with users of an older OneNote

4 Click OK to continue, and the file will be converted and saved

Don't forget

Once you've opened or created a notebook, it will be reopened every time OneNote starts, unless you select File, Info, right-click Settings for the notebook, and select Close.

5 The notebook is no longer in compatibility mode

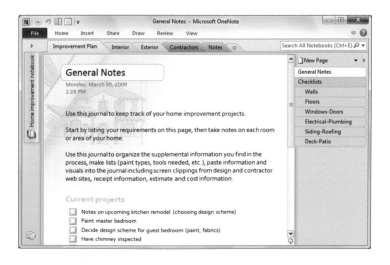

Office Tools

To see which tools are already installed on your system:

1 Select Start, All Programs, Microsoft Office, Microsoft Office Tools, for a list

2 To look for more tools, select Start, Control Panel, and click the link Uninstall a Program

3 Select Microsoft Office 2010, and then click Change

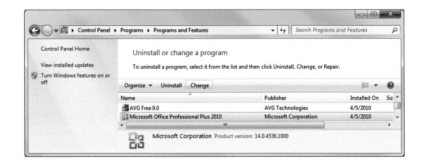

4 Select Add or Remove Features, and click Continue

5 Click [+] to expand the list, click an entry and add it, with Run from my computer (or remove it with Not available)

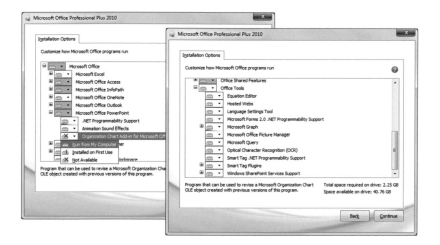

Hot tip

Click a group heading (entries with [+] or [–]) and choose Run All from my computer, to immediately add all the items in that group.

6 When you've selected all that you want, click Continue, the programs will be copied and configured for use

Don't forget

There are also tools in the Shared Features section, which may be selected for installation.

135

7 Click Close to finish setup, when configuration finishes

8 New entries will be added to the Microsoft Office Tools folder in the Start Menu

Picture Manager

This tool helps you manage, edit, and share your pictures, wherever they are located. It can also provide automatic corrections and adjustments, such as red-eye removal.

1 Select Microsoft Office Picture Manager from the Microsoft Office Tools folder in the Start menu

2 Picture Manager shows the image-file contents of your Pictures folder in the Preview pane

3 Click the [+] to expand the folder list, and select a folder from within Pictures, e.g. Photos\Vancouver

4 Drag the Zoom-bar slider to shrink the thumbnails and display more images at a time, or enlarge the thumbnails to display larger (but fewer) images

Hot tip

Picture Manager displays the Shortcuts pane and Task pane, as well as the Preview pane. Use the View command to turn these off (see page 137).

Don't forget

If the folder you select contains no picture files, you'll get an appropriate message. For example, if you select Photos instead of its subfolder, you get:

Hot tip

Click the arrow on the Zoom button to select a specific zoom factor, such as 50% of the usual thumbnail size (or of the full picture size in other views).

50%
800%
400%
200%
150%
100%
50%
25%
12%
Fit

5 Click Filmstrip View on the Views toolbar

6 Click Single Picture View on the Views toolbar

7 To close the Shortcuts and Task panes, click the View command and select the appropriate entry to toggle the setting (or click the [x] at the top right of the Shortcuts or Task pane)

Hot tip

You can change the style of the display in the Preview pane, using the Views toolbar.

Hot tip

The zoom factor in these views is the size of the main image, relative to the full picture size.

137

Don't forget

The View command also allows you to choose the Preview style, and whether to display file names or non-picture-file types.

Edit Pictures

You can adjust the brightness, contrast, and color of your pictures, apply red-eye removal, or crop, resize, rotate, and flip.

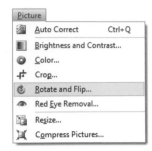

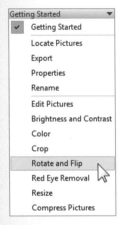

1 Click the Picture command on the menu bar, and select the function that you require, e.g. Rotate and Flip

2 Select the picture or pictures that you want to change

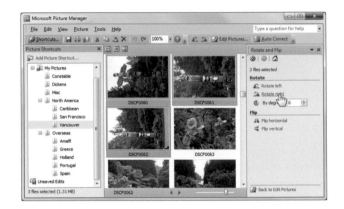

3 Select the subfunction, e.g. Rotate right (defaults to +90°)

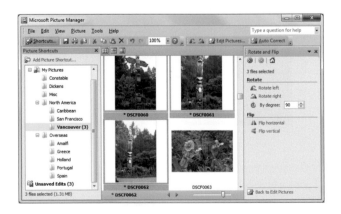

4 Right-click Unsaved Edits and select to Save All (or to Discard All)

Add Picture Shortcuts

If you have picture files in other folders on your hard disk, or on your network, you can add shortcuts to give you quick access, without having to navigate the full path.

1 Select Add Picture Shortcut (on the Shortcuts pane), or Add a new picture shortcut (on the Getting Started Task pane)

2 Navigate to the drive and folder with the pictures that you require, select the folder, and click Add

3 A shortcut to the selected folder will be inserted

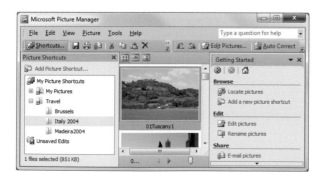

Hot tip

Select Locate pictures in Getting Started, to add shortcuts for all the folders that contain pictures on your system.

Don't forget

You can select folders on any drive on your computer, or on another computer on the same network (as long as you have authorization to share files and folders).

Don't forget

You can add or remove folders, paste files, or rename the shortcut, and all the changes will be reflected in the actual folder, whether it is on the hard disk or the network.

139

Language Preferences

Don't forget

Office supports multiple languages, for editing, for display, for help, and for screen tips.

1 This document includes text in French, which confuses the default English (United States) spelling checker

You'll have similar problems whenever you need to work with documents that have text in other languages, or when you use a system with a different language installed, e.g. when travelling.

To check which languages are enabled, and to add a new language:

Hot tip

You can also set Office language preferences, by selecting File, Options, Language, from within any Office application.

1 From Microsoft Office Tools, on the Start menu, select Office Language Preferences

2 Click the Add Languages box and choose the language

3 Click the Add button, then select any other languages you require, and add those in turn

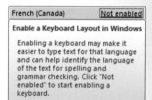

4 Click OK, then OK again to apply the changes, then close and restart any Office applications that are open

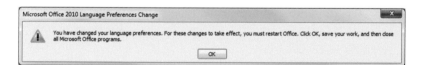

5 Any text in the new languages will normally be detected, and the appropriate spell checker will be employed

Clip Organizer

To make use of Clip Art in an Office application, e.g. PowerPoint:

1 Select the Insert tab and click the Clip Art button (or click Clip Art on the Content bar shown on new slides)

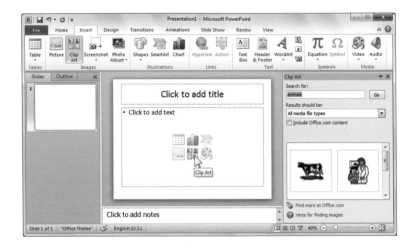

2 On the Clip Art task pane, type a descriptive term and click Go, to search the Office clip art collections.

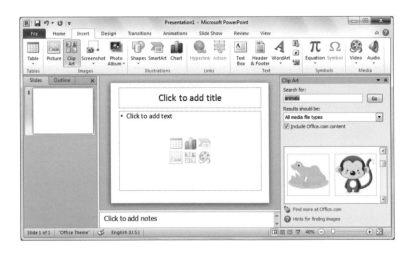

3 Click the box to include the Office.com online clip art, and click Go to repeat the search. In this example, the number of items found increases from 4 to 100.

There's an Office tool to help you build and manage your clip art:

1 Select Microsoft Clip Organizer, from the Microsoft Office Tools folder on the Start menu

Hot tip

The Clip Organizer offers a separate way to run the same software used in the Office applications to find and insert clip art.

2 Click the [+] next to Office Collections to expand the list

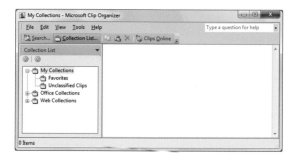

3 Select the Academic category to see thumbnails of the list

143

4 View the Academics category in the Web Collections

Don't forget

For each category, the Clip Organizer shows 4 or 5 items in the Office Collections, or the first 100 of typically 1000 items in that category, in the Web Collections.

Web Collections

To explore the full Web Collections, you can use Search.

1 Click the Search button, enter one or more keywords, and the search characteristics, and click the Go button

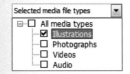

2 Select an item, click the arrow that appears at the right, then select Preview/Properties to see the details

3 Select Make Available Offline from the menu list, to add the item to one of your local collections

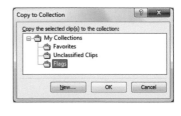

8 Email

The first time you use Outlook, you may need to specify your email account. Then you can receive messages, save attachments, print messages, issue replies, and update your address book, while protecting yourself from spam messages that might be targeted at your account. You can add a standard signature note to your messages. Outlook also helps you subscribe to RSS feeds.

Starting Outlook

Don't forget

Outlook 2010 is found in the Home and Business and the Professional editions of Office 2010.

Hot tip

Windows 7, itself, has no email client, but you can install Windows Live Mail as one of the Windows Live Essentials that you download from the Microsoft website.

The Microsoft Outlook program provides the email and time management functions in Office 2010. To start the application:

1. Select Start, All Programs, Microsoft Office, and select the entry for Microsoft Outlook 2010

To make it quicker and easier to find, you can add it to the top of the Start menu, or to the shortcuts on the taskbar.

1. Locate the Outlook entry, as above, then right-click and select the Pin to Taskbar option

2. Similarly, right-click and select the Pin to Start Menu option, if desired

3. The selected entries will be inserted, and you can select whether to start Outlook

If you had been using another email client, Outlook detects this and issues a prompt:

1. Click Yes to make Outlook the default for email, calendar, and contacts

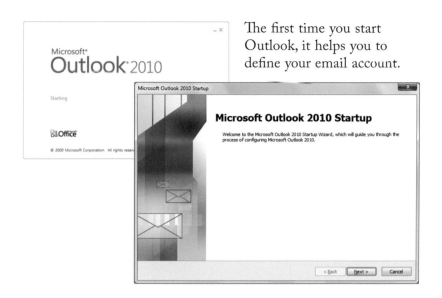

The first time you start Outlook, it helps you to define your email account.

1 Select Yes to configure your email account, and then click Next

2 Type your name, your email address, and your password

Configure Server Settings

Don't forget

Your connection to the Internet must be active at this time, so that the wizard can make the connection.

1 The wizard identifies your Internet connection, and establishes the network connection

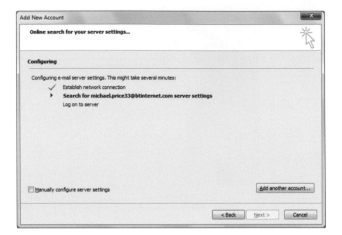

2 The wizard then searches for the server settings that support your email account

Hot tip

This illustrates the process for the POP3 email account, the standard type. You may need to select the manual configuration for other types of server, using the information provided by your email supplier.

3 Finally, the wizard logs on to the server, using your account name and password, and sends a test message

4 Click Finish and your email account will be configured, ready for use

Your First Messages

Outlook opens with the Inbox, showing your first email messages, e.g. welcome messages from the ISP, or the Outlook test message.

Quick Access Toolbar   Tab bar   Title bar   Help

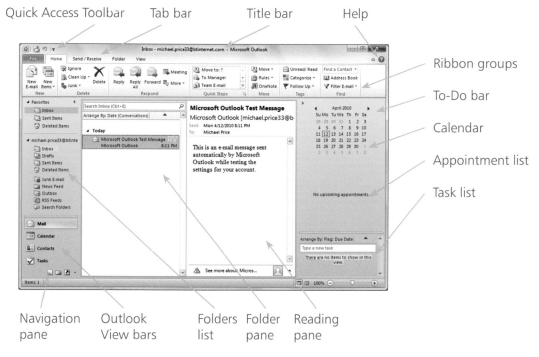

Ribbon groups

To-Do bar

Calendar

Appointment list

Task list

Navigation pane   Outlook View bars   Folders list   Folder pane   Reading pane

You may collapse the Navigation pane and the To-Do bar, to provide more space to display your longer messages.

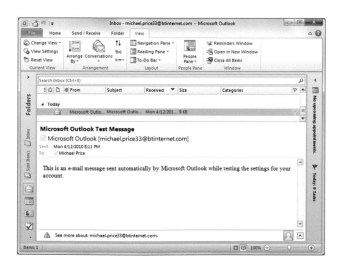

Hot tip

These illustrations show the Reading Pane in use (the default setting). However, you may prefer to turn this off (see page 150) to avoid potential problems with spam and phishing emails.

You may also have the Reading Pane below the message list.

Turn Off Reading Pane

1 Select View, Reading Pane, and choose Off, rather than Right or Bottom

2 Messages will now be left unread, until you explicitly open them

Hot tip

It is possible that the very act of reading an email message could release harmful software into your system. Turning off the Reading pane allows you to review the message source and title before it is actually read.

150

Don't forget

Messages are shown arranged by date, and shown in groups. You can change the view, to sort by sender or subject for example.

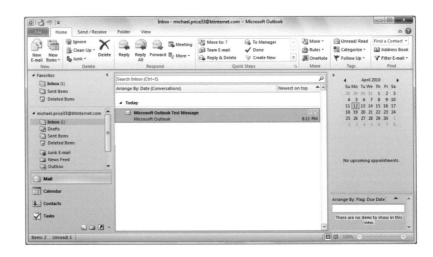

3 Double-click (or select and Enter) to open a message

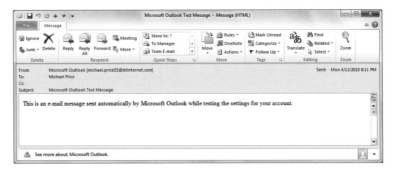

4 When the message has been opened, its entry in the Inbox folder is shown in regular, rather than bold font

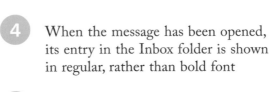

5 Select File and Close, or click the Close button, or press Alt+F4 to exit

Request a Newsletter

You'll need to share your email address with friends, contacts, and organizations, to begin exchanging messages. You can also use your email address to request newsletters. For example:

1 Visit the website www.perryweb.com/dickens

2 Scroll down to the hyperlink Get Our Newsletter and click on it

3 Enter your email address, re-enter it to confirm, and then click Subscribe

4 Your email address is added to the list, and an email inviting you to accept the subscription will be sent to you

5 Check your Inbox periodically for the confirmation message

6 Double-click the email confirmation request message when it arrives in your Inbox

Don't forget

Your address could be provided, accidently or deliberately, without your permission, so you must explicitly confirm your wishes.

7 Select the link provided, to confirm you issued the request

Hot tip

Retain this email, since it provides the links needed to change your details, or to unsubscribe, if you no longer wish to receive the newsletter.

8 Another email will arrive, completing the subscription

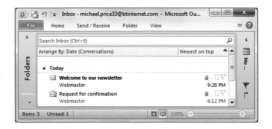

Receive a Message

To check for any mail that may be waiting:

1 Open Outlook, select the Send/Receive tab, and click the Send/Receive button

Send/Receive
All Folders

Hot tip

Depending on the settings, Outlook may automatically issue a Send/Receive when it starts up, and at intervals thereafter.

2 New mail will be downloaded and displayed in the Inbox

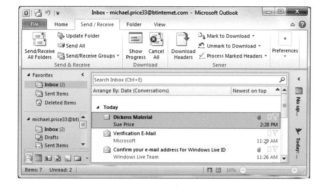

3 Double-click the message title to display the contents

Don't forget

Your messages may have an attachment that has a certification that a virus check has been applied. This is added by your antivirus software. You can usually turn off such notifications.

Certification.txt (265 B)

4 Right-click one of the attachments, and then select Save As to save that particular attachment

5 Specify the target folder (see page 154) and choose Save

London Map.jpg (102 KB)
- Preview
- Open
- Quick Print
- Save As
- Save All Attachments...
- Remove Attachment
- Copy Attachments
- Select All

Save All Attachments

To save all the attachments at once:

1 Open the message, right-click any attachment, and select Save All Attachments

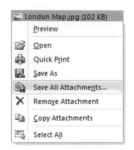

2 The list of attachments is displayed, with all the attachments selected

3 Press Ctrl, and click any of the attachments to adjust the selection, then click OK to download

4 Locate the folder to receive the downloads (or click New Folder to insert a new folder), then click OK to save

Print the Message

1 From the message, select the File tab, then click Print

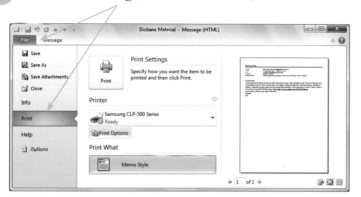

2 You can change the printer or adjust the print settings, for example, change the number of copies required

3 If you click in the Print options box, you will also print the attached files

4 For picture attachments, you can choose the print size

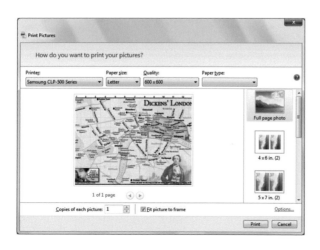

Hot tip

The File Print Preview shows how the message will appear on the page. Select Quick Print to send the message to the printer, using all the default settings.

Beware

Each attachment will print as a separate print job, destined for the default printer. You can change the printer and the print size on each job, but you cannot combine the prints onto the same sheet.

Reply to the Message

1 When you want to reply to a message that you've opened, click the Reply button, in the Respond group on the Message tab

2 The message form opens with the email address, the subject entered, and the cursor in the message area, ready for you to type your comments above the original text

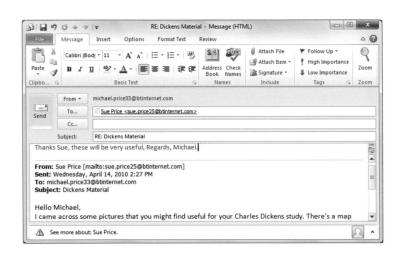

3 Complete your response and then click the Send button

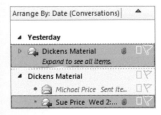

The Reading Pane may be active, even if switched off in the Inbox, since it must be separately configured for each folder

Add Address to Contacts

Whenever you receive an email, you can add the sender (and any other addressees) to your Outlook Contacts list

1 Right-click the email address and select Add to Outlook Contacts

2 Add any extra information you have, and then click Save & Close

3 Select the Contacts folder to create and update entries

Spam and Phishing

As useful as email can be, it does have problem areas. Because it is so cheap and easy to use, the criminally inclined take advantage of email for their own profit. They send out thousands of spam (junk email) messages, in the hope of getting one or two replies.

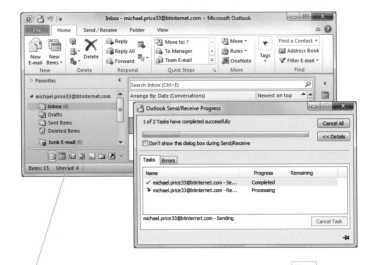

158

Hot tip

Any message sent to the Junk Email folder is converted to plain-text format, and all links are disabled. In addition, the Reply and Reply All functions are disabled.

> Links and other functionality have been disabled in this message. To restore functionality, move this message to the Inbox. This message was converted to plain text.

The Outlook Junk Email filter identifies spam, and moves the messages to the Junk Email folder. To adjust the settings:

1 From the Home tab, select the Junk button in the Delete group, then click Junk Email Options

2 Select your desired level of protection: No Automatic Filtering, Low (default), High or Safe Lists Only

3 Click the appropriate tab, to specify lists of safe senders, safe recipients or blocked senders and international domains

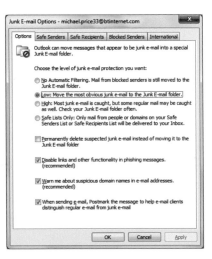

Don't forget

You can block messages from specified top level domain codes, and messages in particular foreign languages.

Outlook also provides protection for the Inbox:

1 Links to pictures on the sender's website may be blocked

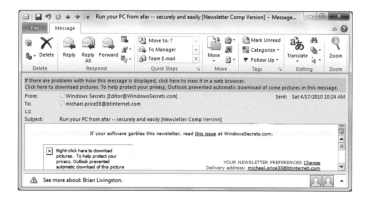

2 Links to websites may be disabled, and you may not be allowed to use the Reply and Reply All functions

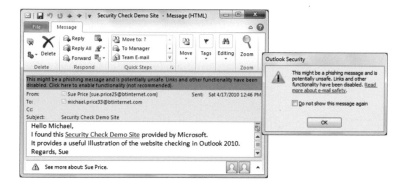

3 Even if you over-ride the block, the link may still get intercepted by Internet Explorer's check for phishing sites

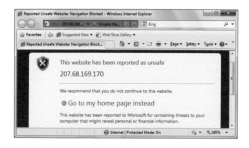

Create a Message

1 Select the Mail folder, and then click the New button to open a new mail message form

2 Click the To button to open the address book

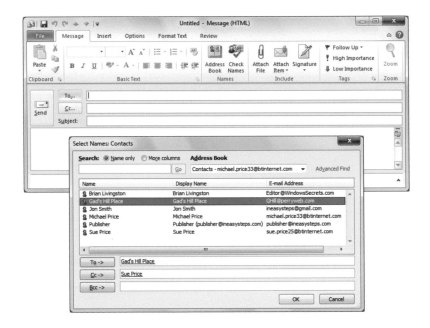

3 Select the addressee and click To, then click OK

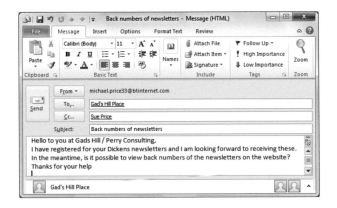

4 Type the subject, greeting, and text for your message

Insert a Signature

You can create a standard signature, to add to the emails you send.

1 Select the Insert tab and click Signature in the Include group, then click Signatures

2 Click the New button, specify a name for the new signature, then click OK

New Signature

Type a name for this signature:

Freelance Author

OK   Cancel

New

3 Add the text required, and click OK to save the signature

4 When you've added one or more, click Signature again and select a signature to insert into the message, at the typing cursor location

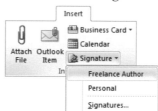

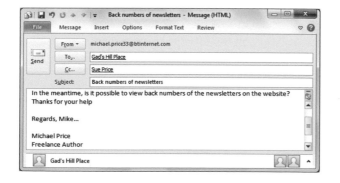

Color Categories

You can use color to help sort and organize your messages.

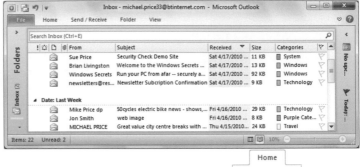

Hot tip

Select the Minimize button to minimize the Navigation pane, or the To-Do bar, to make more space for the message properties.

To associate a color with a message:

1 Select the message, click the Categorize button in the toolbar, and choose the applicable color

2 The first time you select a specific color, you'll be asked if you want to rename it, or assign it a shortcut key

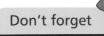

Don't forget

Choose Set Quick Click, to define the color category to be assigned when you single-click the Categories column.

3 Select All Categories to assign more than one category to a message, or to add, rename, or delete categories

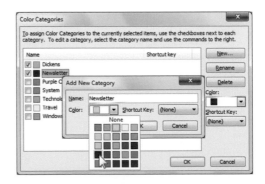

RSS Feeds

RSS (Really Simple Syndication) is a way for publishers of Internet data to make news, blogs, and other information available to subscribers. You can add feeds and view subscriptions in either Internet Explorer or Outlook. To synchronize these programs:

1 Click File, Open, Import, then select Import RSS Feeds from the Common Feed List, and click Next

2 Select the feeds to add to Outlook (or Select All) and click Next, and then Finish

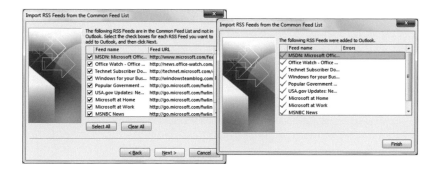

3 To ensure that the programs remain synchronized, select File, Options, Advanced, and then Synchronize RSS Feeds

Don't forget

The Common Feed List is a list of subscribed RSS Feeds saved as part of your user profile, and used by RSS client programs, including Outlook and Internet Explorer.

Hot tip

If you have previously subscribed to RSS feeds in Internet Explorer, you'll also need to add these to Outlook.

...cont'd

Hot tip

Subscribing to RSS feeds from Internet Explorer is the quickest and easiest way to add RSS feeds to Outlook.

Hot tip

Select a feed name, and the list of items is displayed, the highlighted item is then shown in the Reading Pane.

4   When you subscribe to a new feed in Internet Explorer, it is added to the Common Feed List

5   Select Mail, RSS Feeds, and double-click to expand, you'll see the new feed in Outlook

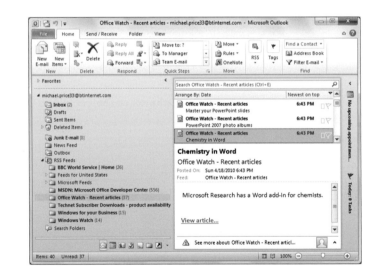

6   Click the white triangle to expand the folder

7   When the feed name is shown in Bold, you know it contains unread items

8   The number of unread items is in parentheses after the name, and changes as items are downloaded or read

9 Time Management

Outlook is much more than an email manager. It is a complete personal information management system, with full diary and calendar facilities. It enables you to keep track of appointments and meetings, and to control and schedule your tasks. You can keep notes, make journal entries, and correlate all these with email messages relating to those records.

Outlook Calendar

The Outlook Calendar handles time-based activities, including appointments, meetings, holidays, courses, and events (single-day or multi-day). It provides a high-level view by day, week, or month and will give you reminders when an activity is due. To open:

 Click the Calendar button on the Navigation pane

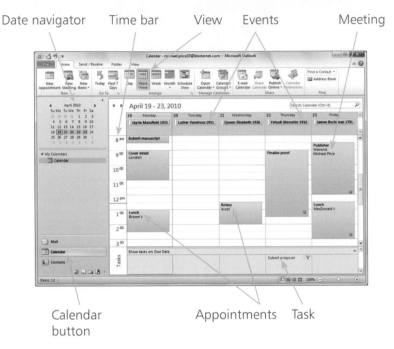

Date navigator   Time bar   View   Events   Meeting

Calendar button   Appointments   Task

You can also view current calendar events on the Today page:

 Select the Mail button and click Personal Folders

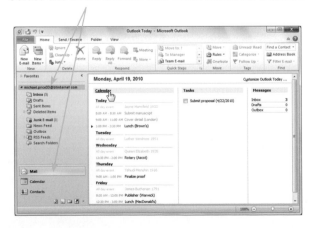

Schedule an Appointment

An appointment reserves space in your calendar for an activity that does not involve inviting other people, or for reserving resources.

1 Open the Calendar (day, week, or month view) and use the date navigator to select the day for the appointment

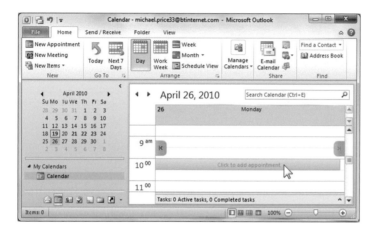

2 Move the mouse pointer over the time when the appointment should begin, then click as prompted

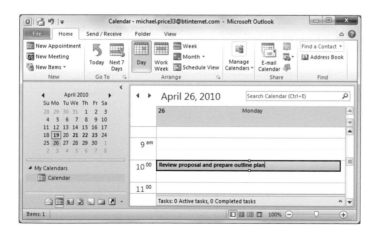

3 Type the subject, then drag the handle on the lower edge, to extend the appointment to the required duration

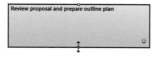

Hot tip

If the large Calendar button is hidden, click the small calendar button at the foot of the Navigation pane.

167

Don't forget

You can drag the handle on the top edge to adjust the starting time for the appointment.

Change Appointment Details

You can change and add to the information stored in the calendar.

You can select New Appointment from the Start menu, or Taskbar Jump List (see page 160), and provide all of the details, including date and time.

1 Double-click the appointment to open the appointment editor form, showing the information provided so far

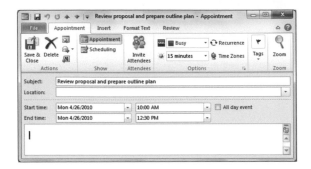

2 Add or change details, such as the start time, end time, location, or description, as needed, then click Save & Close

Hot tip

By default, you will get a reminder popup for the appointment 15 minutes before the start time, or you can set your own notice period.

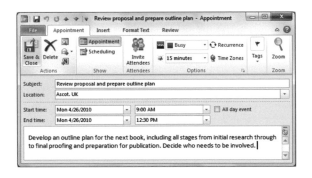

3 The appointment is displayed in your calendar, alongside any other entries for that time of day

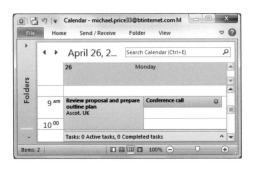

Recurring Appointments

When you have an activity that's repeated on a regular basis, you can define it as a recurring appointment.

1 Open the appointments form and specify the details for a first occurrence of the activity, then click Recurrence

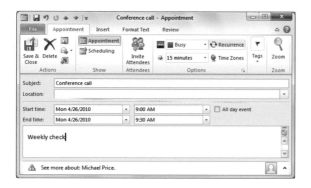

2 Specify how often the activity will be repeated, and over what range of time it should take place

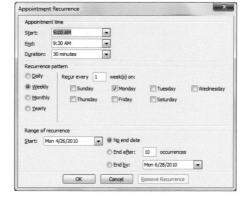

3 Click OK, and then click Save & Close to record the changes

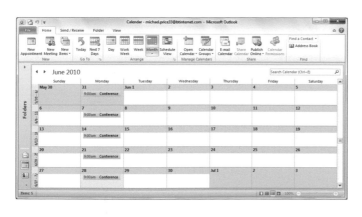

169

Hot tip

You can take an existing appointment, or meeting, and click Recurrence to make it a recurring activity.

Beware

Unless you limit the number of recurrences, or set a termination date, the activity will be scheduled for all possible days in the future.

Don't forget

All the occurrences of the activity will now be displayed in the calendar, on the appropriate days. If there's room, the recurrence symbol will appear after the subject.

Create a Meeting

1 Double-click the appointment entry in the calendar, and click the Invite Attendees button in the Attendees group

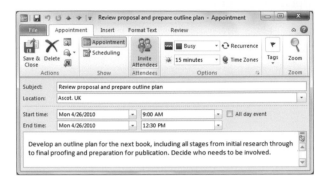

2 On the invitation message form displayed, click the To button to open the contacts address list

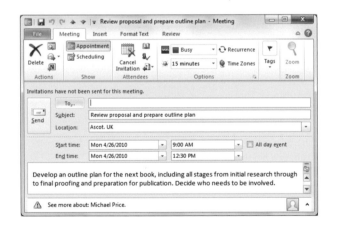

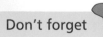
3 Select the email address for each attendee, in turn, and click the Required or the Optional button, as appropriate, then click OK

4 When all the attendees have been added, click the Send button to send the invitation to each of them

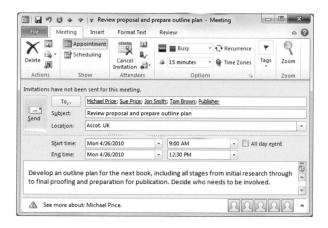

5 The invitation will be received in the organizer's Inbox

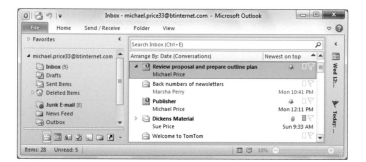

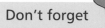

Don't forget

You can also display the meeting record, and view the current status, by double-clicking the meeting entry in your calendar.

6 Opening this message displays the meeting record, with the latest status. The organizer is not required to respond

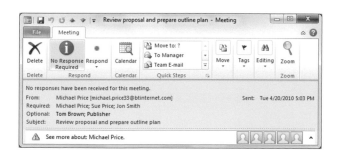

Respond to an Invitation

Beware

The attendees must be using a version of Outlook in order to be able to properly receive and respond to meeting invitations.

Hot tip

You can click the Tentative button to accept provisionally.

1 When other attendees receive and open the invitation, it provides buttons to accept, decline, or to propose a new time

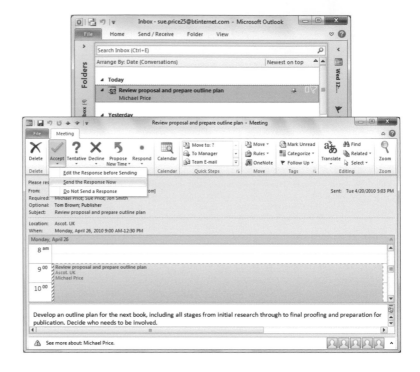

2 Click Accept, then OK, to send your response and add the appointment to your calendar

3 The original message is removed from the Inbox, and the response is inserted into the Sent box

Don't forget

You can edit the response, if desired, or you can accept the invitation without sending a response. It will simply be added to your calendar.

4 The originator receives responses from attendees, as emails

5 The message shows the attendee's response and status

6 The meeting record displays the updated status

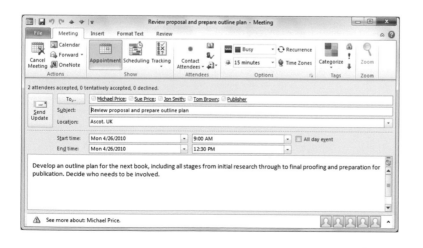

Don't forget

The message shows the current status, so it will show the latest information each time it is opened.

173

Hot tip

Any changes that the originator makes to the meeting details will be sent to the attendees as update messages.

Report Free/Busy Time

Outlook can help you choose the most suitable times to hold meetings, based on reports from the proposed attendees, giving details of their availability.

To publish this information, each attendee should:

Hot tip

Sharing free/busy information relies on attendees, and the meeting coordinator, having access to a drive, a file server on the network, or pages on a web server.

1 Open Outlook, select File and then Options

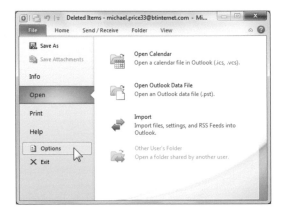

2 In Outlook Options, select Calendar then click the Free/Busy Options button in the Calendar Options

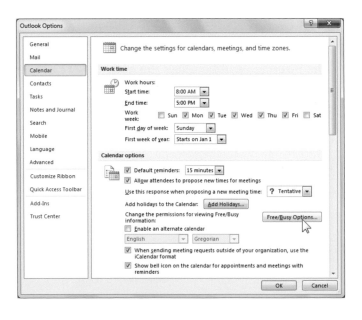

Don't forget

Scroll down and click the Resource Scheduling button to set up a calendar for coordinating resources, such as conference rooms and projector equipment.

Resource scheduling

3 Click the box labelled Publish at my location

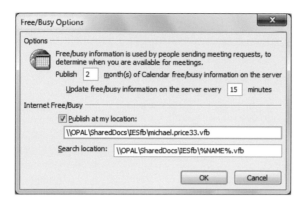

Hot tip

You can specify how much information to provide, and how often to issue updates. By default, details will be published covering the next two months, and updates will be recorded every 15 minutes.

4 Provide the path to the shared location, the Shared Documents folder on a networked computer in this example

5 For potential meeting originators only, put the same path, with %NAME% as the username, to search for any user

6 Click OK to initiate the reporting

Don't forget

The free/busy data is stored in a .vfb file, with the file name the same as the username section of your email account.

The file will be stored in the specified location, and will be updated at the specified frequency.

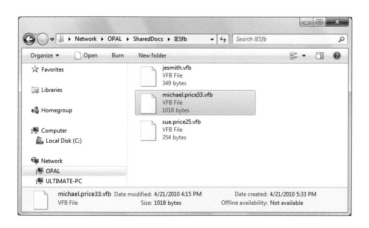

Files for the other attendees who choose to publish their busy and free time details will also be found here.

Schedule a Meeting

You can use the reported free/busy information to help set up a meeting. For example, to reschedule a meeting you've just set up:

1 Create a meeting (see page 170) with initial details, such as expected start, duration, and proposed attendees

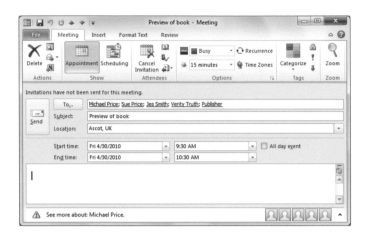

2 Click Scheduling, to show free/busy times, and click AutoPick Next to see the next available time slot

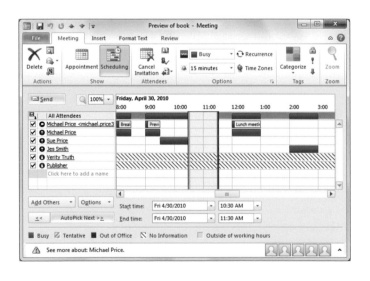

3 Click Send to add the revised details to your calendar, and to send an invitation (or an update) to all the attendees

Add Holidays

To make sure that your calendar is an accurate reflection of your availability, add details of national holidays and similar events.

1 Select File, Options, Calendar (see page 174), then click the Add Holidays button in the Calendar options

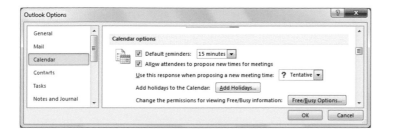

(see page 174)

2 Select the countries that you wish to add, then click OK and click OK again to finish

3 To see the new entries that have been added, open the Calendar, select the View tab, then click Change View, List

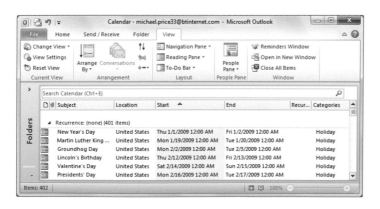

Hot tip

By default, no holidays or special events are shown in your Calendar, but Outlook does have a holiday file, with information for 88 countries and events for the years 2009–2028.

Don't forget

Your own country or region is automatically selected the first time you choose the Add Holidays option.

177

Hot tip

If you have more than one country inserted, you can click Location to sort the events into country groupings. Use this, for example, to remove events for one country.

Creating Tasks

To create an implicit task:

1 Right-click an Outlook item (for example, a message or contact), select Follow Up and select the flag for the timing

2 The follow-up item is added to the Task folder, and also appears on the To-Do bar

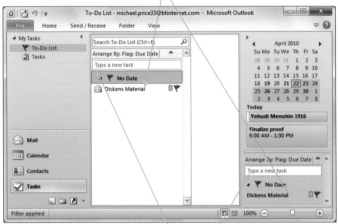

To create an explicit task:

1 Click the prompt "Type a new task" in the Task folder, or on the To-Do bar

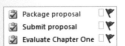

2 Type the subject for the task, and then press Enter

3 The task is inserted into the Tasks folder, with the default characteristics (current date for the start and the due dates, and no reminder time set)

To make changes to the details for the task:

1 Double-click on the task entry on the To-Do bar, or in the Task folder

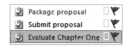

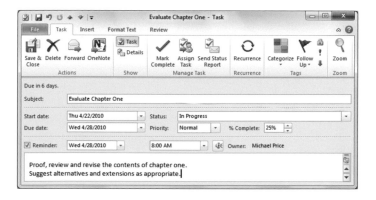

2 You can change the start date or the due date, add a description, apply a reminder, update the priority, or indicate how much has been completed

179

3 When you update the %Complete, the status changes to In progress or Complete, or click the down-arrow to choose an alternative status value

4 Click the Details button in the Show group to add information about carrying out the task, e.g. hours worked

Assigning Tasks

You can define a task that someone else is to perform, assign it to that person and get status reports and updates on its progress.

To assign an existing task:

1 Open the task and click the Assign Task button, found in the Manage Task group

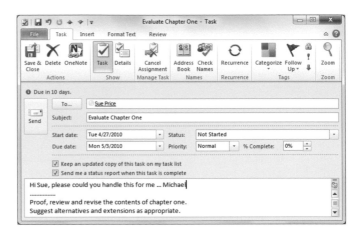

180

2 In the To box, type the name or email address, or click the To button and select an entry from the Contacts list

3 Click Send, to initiate the task-assignment request, then click OK to confirm the new ownership

4 The message will be sent, with a copy stored in the Sent Items folder

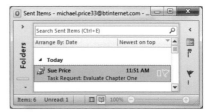

Accepting Task Requests

1 The task details on the originating system shows that it is awaiting a response from the recipient of the task request

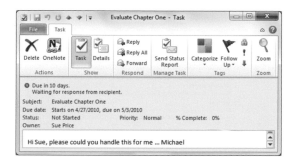

2 The task request appears in the recipient's Inbox

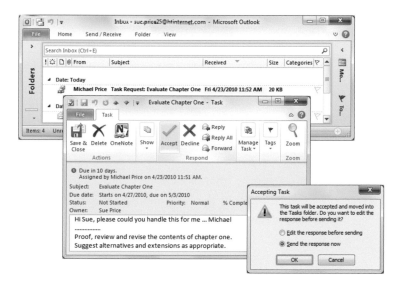

Hot tip

If the task is rejected, ownership is returned to the originator, who can then assign the task to another person.

3 The recipient opens the message, clicks the Accept button, then clicks OK to send the response

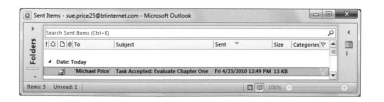

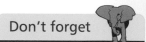

Don't forget

The task request is sent to the originator, and a copy is saved in the Sent Items folder.

Confirming the Assignment

1 The response appears in the originator's Inbox, as a message from the recipient of the task request

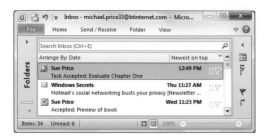

2 When the message is opened, it shows the task with its change of ownership

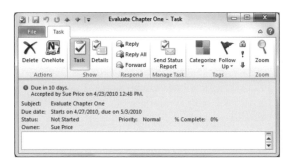

Don't forget

The originator is no longer able to make changes to the task details, since ownership has been transferred to the recipient.

3 The task appears in the originator's Tasks folder, listed under the new owner's name

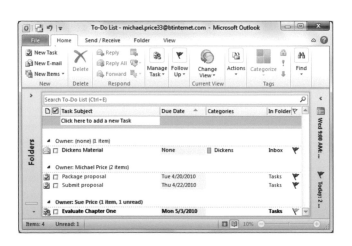

4 The new owner can change task details, and click Save & Close to save them, as the task progresses

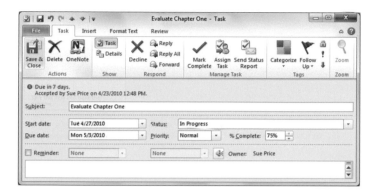

5 When finished, the task can be marked as complete

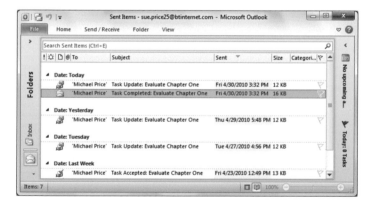

6 For each change, the originator is sent an update message, to change the details of the task in the task folder

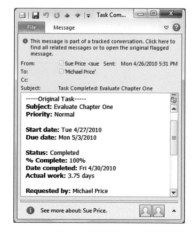

7 When the task is finally completed, the originator receives a status report, with hours worked, if recorded (see page 179)

Notes

You may need a prompt, but the activity doesn't justify creating a task or an appointment. In such a case, you can use Outlook Notes. To create a note from anywhere in Outlook:

1. Select the Home tab, click the New items button, and select More Items, then Note (or press the shortcut Ctrl+Shift+N)

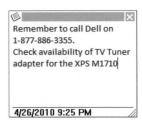

2. Type the text for your note in the form that's displayed, and it will be added to the Notes folder

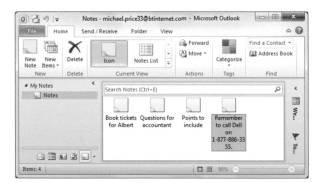

3. Open the Notes folder from the navigation pane to see the current set of notes stored there

4. The note titles may be truncated, so select a note to see its full title – the text up to the first Enter, or else the whole text, if there's no Enter symbol

5 Click Small Icons to allow more space for the note title

Hot tip

Using category colors, you can associate different types of Outlook items that are all concerned with the same subject or topic.

6 Right-click a note to select Categorize, and assign a color category (see page 162) to that particular note

To change the default settings for new notes that you create:

1 Select the File tab, then click Options, and then select Notes and Journal

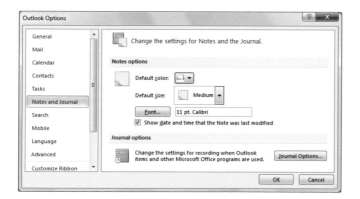

Don't forget

Settings offer three sizes of note, but you can click and drag an edge or corner to make a note any size you wish.

2 You can specify the color (blue, green, pink, yellow, or white), the size (small, medium, or large) and font attributes

These changes will apply to your future notes only – they will not be applied to the existing notes in the Notes folder.

185

Journal

Outlook can automatically record information about activities related to Outlook items in the Journal, a type of project log book.

1 Select Journal from the navigation pane (or press the shortcut keys Ctrl+8)

 Journal

2 If Journal is currently not active, you'll be reminded of other ways to track activities

3 Click Yes to turn the Journal on

4 Select Journal Options for items, contacts, and Office file types to be recorded, then OK

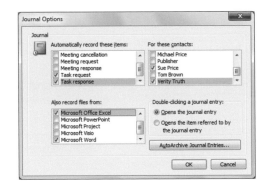

5 The Journal begins to record the specified data, in a timeline format, as shown in the example below.

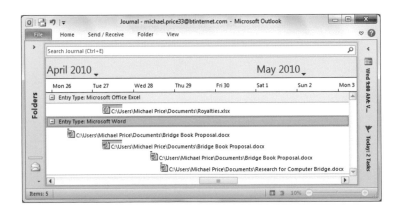

10 Manage Files

It is useful to understand how Office manages the files that constitute the documents, so that you can choose the appropriate formats when you share documents with other users.

Windows 7 Versus XP

Despite the visual contrasts between Windows XP, the newer Windows Vista, and Windows 7, most operations in Office will be the same. However, file management does exhibit important differences.

Although most features of Office 2010 are independent of the actual version of Windows you are using, there are differences to watch out for, when managing files and folders.

To illustrate the variations between the systems:

1 Open Word 2010 in Windows XP, then select File, and then click Open

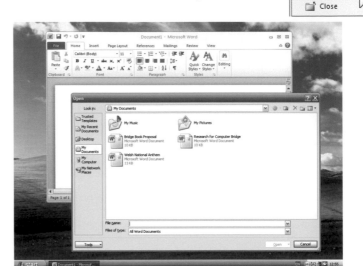

2 Repeat the same actions for Word 2010 in Windows 7

This shows the results with Windows 7 and Aero. The results will be similar for Windows Vista. The Home Basic editions of these systems are functionally the same, but do not display the transparency effects.

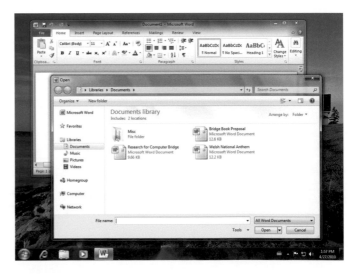

These screenshots show some minor differences. For example:

- Office documents are in My Documents folder in XP, and in the Documents library in 7/Vista

- Access to the drives on your system is via My Computer in XP, and Computer in 7/Vista

- Networked drives are found in My Network Places for XP, and in Network for 7/Vista

- XP, unlike 7/Vista, has no direct access to the operating-system file and folder search facilities

To see where the documents and computer folders are located:

1 In XP, select Start, All Programs, Accessories, Windows Explorer, then open My Computer, C:, Documents and Settings, the current username, and then My Documents

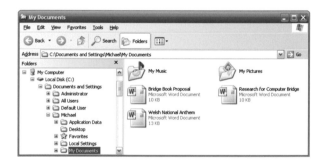

2 In Windows 7/Vista, expand the entries for Computer, Users, current user name, and select the Documents folder

189

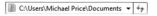

Finding Files

The search facilities are one of the strengths of Windows 7/Vista, and Office 2010 takes full advantage of them. To illustrate this, suppose you've created a document discussing the Stayman bridge convention, but appear to have saved it in the wrong folder.

To track it down, when using Office 2010 with Windows 7:

 Hot tip

Select Documents, or choose another folder or drive where you expect to find your missing document.

1 Open Word 2010 and click the File tab button, then select Open

2 Click in the Search box, and type the search terms, for example, Stayman

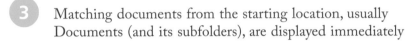

3 Matching documents from the starting location, usually Documents (and its subfolders), are displayed immediately

 Beware

Any documents that contain the specified word in their titles, or in their contents, will be selected.

190

 Don't forget

This shows that the required document has been misfiled in the Misc folder within Documents.

4 Select the Content view to see details of the files, including parts of the text and the full path

5 Right-click a file, and select Open file location, to see the folder where it is stored

6 Double-click the file entry to open it in Word, to view or edit the contents

To locate the document when you are using Office 2010 with Windows XP, you must use the operating system Search facility:

1 Click the Start button, and select Search on the Start menu

2 Select All files and folders, then specify the file type, a word from the contents, and the location to start from

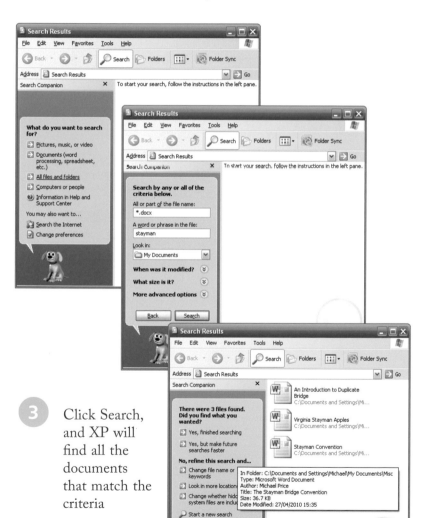

3 Click Search, and XP will find all the documents that match the criteria

Don't forget

Although Word has been used for this example, the same search procedures apply for documents in other Office applications, for example, Excel and PowerPoint.

Beware

In the XP search, you'll need separate searches to locate documents with the specified word in their titles, or in their textual contents.

Don't forget

Hold the mouse pointer over a document icon, and the tooltip will show where the document is stored.

Recent Documents

When you want to return to a file that you viewed recently, you may be able to select it from the list of recently-used documents.

1 Select the File tab, click Recent, if not already selected, and review the entries in the Recent Documents list

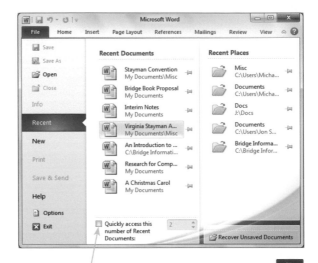

2 Click the Quick Access box, to list the first few documents on the File tab menu

3 To change the number of entries that are displayed on the list, click File, Options

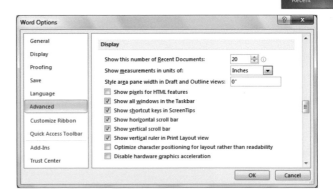

4 Click Advanced, scroll down to the Display options, then set the number of recent documents desired, and click OK

To change the file types listed when you open documents:

1 Select the File tab button and click Open

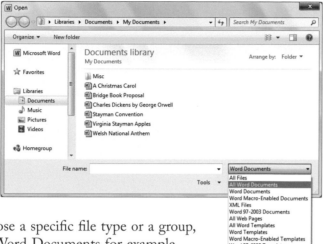

2 Choose a specific file type or a group, All Word Documents for example

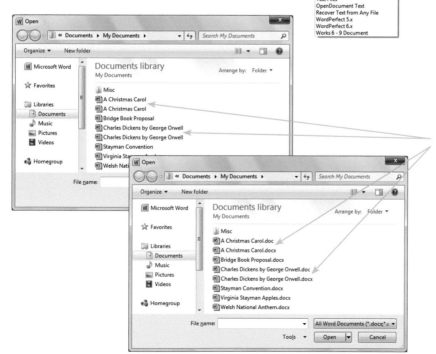

3 You'll need to change Folder Options (see page 20) to show the file extensions for the file types you've selected

XML File Formats

Office 2010 uses file formats based on XML, first introduced in Office 2007. They apply to Word 2010, Excel 2010, and PowerPoint 2010. The XML file types include:

Application	XML file type	Extension
Word	Document	.docx
	Macro-enabled document	.docm
	Template	.dotx
	Macro-enabled template	.dotm
Excel	Workbook	.xlsx
	Macro-enabled workbook	.xlsm
	Template	.xltx
	Macro-enabled template	.xltm
	Non-XML binary workbook	.xlsb
	Macro-enabled add-in	.xlam
PowerPoint	Presentation	.pptx
	Macro-enabled presentation	.pptm
	Template	.potx
	Macro-enabled template	.potm
	Macro-enabled add-in	.ppam
	Show	.ppsx
	Macro-enabled show	.ppsm
	Slide	.sldx
	Macro-enabled slide	.sldm
	Office theme	.thmx

The benefits of using the new file formats are:

- Document Size

The new formats are automatically compressed, and can be up to 75% smaller, saving disk space and reducing transmission sizes and times when you send files via email, over networks, or across the Internet.

- Document Recovery

Files are structured in a modular fashion, which keeps different data components in the file separate from each other. This allows files

Hot tip

This is all, automatically handled. You do not have to install any special zip utilities to open and close files in Office 2010.

to be opened, even if a component within the file (for example, a chart or table) is damaged or corrupted (see page 202).

● Macro Management

Files saved using the default x suffix (such as .docx, .xlsx, and .pptx) cannot contain executable Visual Basic for Applications (VBA) macros, or XML macros. Only files using the m suffix (e.g. .docm, .xlsm, and .pptm) can contain such macros.

● Privacy

Personally identifiable information and business-sensitive information, such as author names, comments, tracked changes, and file paths, can be identified and removed using Document Inspector (see page 212).

Compatibility

To maintain compatibility, Office 2010 can read, edit and save files in the original binary file formats used by older versions of Office. This allows you to create documents in formats other users can work with, even if they don't have Office 2010.

Alternatively, those users can download the Compatibility Pack:

1 Go to www.microsoft.com/downloads and search for the Microsoft Office Compatibility Pack

2 Click Download, and follow the prompts to download and install the file-format converters

Don't forget

This means that you can avoid receiving files with hidden and unexpected macros, which could otherwise potentially affect the integrity of your data.

Beware

For the converters to work, the users must update their versions of Microsoft Office to the appropriate service level:
Office 2000 SP3
Office XP SP3
Office 2003 SP1

Hot tip

With these converters, users of older versions of Office can create, edit, and save documents in the new XML formats.

195

Save As PDF or XPS

There are times when you'd like to allow other users to view and print your documents, but you'd rather they didn't make changes. These could include résumés, legal documents, newsletters, or any other documents that are meant for review only. Office 2010 provides for this situation, with two built-in file formats.

Portable Document Format (PDF)

PDF is a fixed-layout file format that preserves your document formatting when the file is viewed online or printed, while the data in the file cannot be easily changed. The PDF format is also useful for documents that will be published, using commercial printing methods.

XML Paper Specification (XPS)

XPS also preserves document formatting and protects the data content. However, it is not yet widely used. The XPS format ensures that, when the file is viewed online or printed, it retains the exact format you intended, and that data in the file cannot be easily changed.

To save an Office document in either format:

Hot tip

PDF was developed, and is supported by, Adobe, which provides a free Reader for viewing and printing PDF files. XPS is a competitive product from Microsoft, who also provide a free XPS viewer.

1. Open the document in the appropriate application, for example, open a Word document using Word 2010

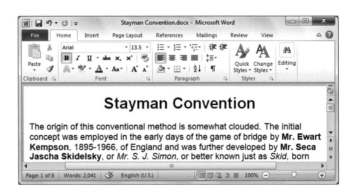

Don't forget

All the Office 2010 applications include the capability to save documents or reports in the PDF and XPS formats.

2. Make any required changes to the document, then select the File tab

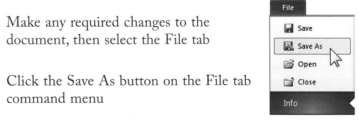

3. Click the Save As button on the File tab command menu

4 Click the Save as type box, and select PDF or XPS format

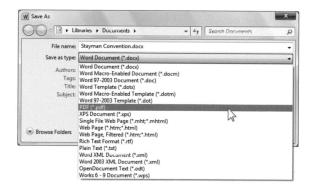

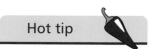

Hot tip

By default, the file will be saved in the selected format in the same folder as the original document.

5 Select Standard or Online quality, and then click Save

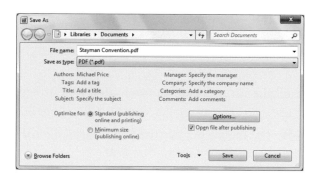

Don't forget

You can optimize the document for online viewing or for printing, and you can choose to open the file after it has been stored.

6 The document is saved to disk in the required format, and then displayed using Adobe Reader or XPS Viewer

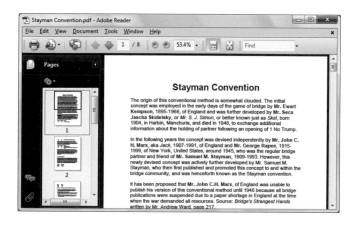

Beware

If you are running Office 2010 under Windows XP, you may be required to download the XPS Viewer. This is already included in Windows 7.

Fonts in Office 2010

There are a number of new fonts provided with Windows 7 and Office 2010, including Calibri, Cambria, Candara, Consolas, Constantia, Corbel, Nyala, and Segoe. You can preview text using these fonts, or any other of the Windows fonts:

1 From the Home tab, select the text to be previewed, click the down-arrow on the Font box

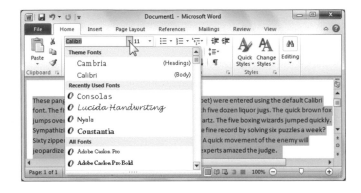

2 Scroll the list to locate an interesting font, if necessary

3 Move the mouse pointer over the font name to see an immediate preview using that font

4 Click on the desired font name to put the change into effect

This helps indicate how the text will appear, but is an awkward way to explore the large number of fonts available.

With the help of a macro available from Microsoft, you can create a document that provides a sample of every font on your system.

1 Visit support.microsoft.com/kb/209205

2 Scroll down to ListAllFonts, and select the code

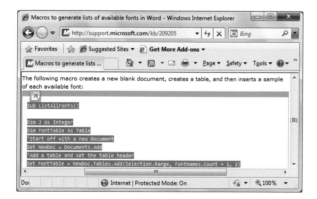

3 Open a new blank document, and select the View tab, ready to work with macros

Create and Run ListAllFonts

1 Click the arrow on the Macros button in the Macros group, and select the View Macros entry

2 Name the macro ListAllFonts, choose Macros in Document1, and click Create

3 Highlight the skeleton code

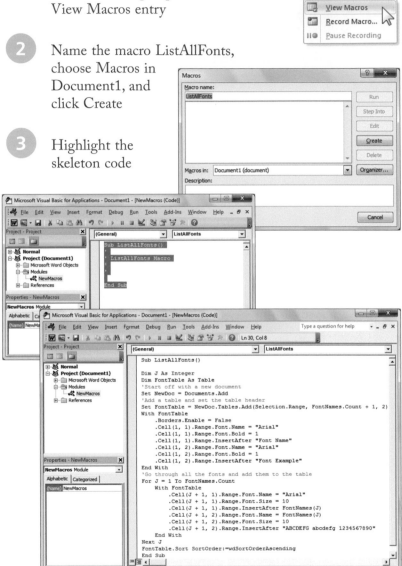

```
Sub ListAllFonts()

Dim J As Integer
Dim FontTable As Table
'Start off with a new document
Set NewDoc = Documents.Add
'Add a table and set the table header
Set FontTable = NewDoc.Tables.Add(Selection.Range, FontNames.Count + 1, 2)
With FontTable
    .Borders.Enable = False
    .Cell(1, 1).Range.Font.Name = "Arial"
    .Cell(1, 1).Range.Font.Bold = 1
    .Cell(1, 1).Range.InsertAfter "Font Name"
    .Cell(1, 2).Range.Font.Name = "Arial"
    .Cell(1, 2).Range.Font.Bold = 1
    .Cell(1, 2).Range.InsertAfter "Font Example"
End With
'Go through all the fonts and add them to the table
For J = 1 To FontNames.Count
    With FontTable
        .Cell(J + 1, 1).Range.Font.Name = "Arial"
        .Cell(J + 1, 1).Range.Font.Size = 10
        .Cell(J + 1, 1).Range.InsertAfter FontNames(J)
        .Cell(J + 1, 2).Range.Font.Name = FontNames(J)
        .Cell(J + 1, 2).Range.Font.Size = 10
        .Cell(J + 1, 2).Range.InsertAfter "ABCDEFG abcdefg 1234567890"
    End With
Next J
FontTable.Sort SortOrder:=wdSortOrderAscending
End Sub
```

4 Copy and paste the code from the Microsoft website, then select File, Close, and Return to Microsoft Word

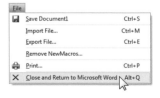

5 Reselect View Macros, click the macro name, and then click Run

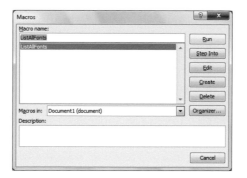

6 A new document is created, and the font samples are inserted

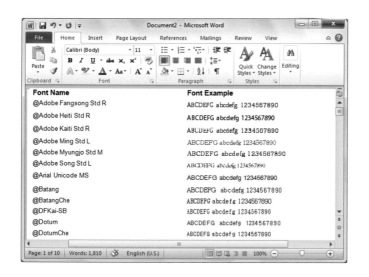

7 Save the document, to keep the list of font samples for future reference

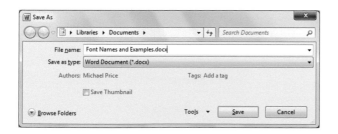

8 If you want to keep a copy of the macro, you will need to save the first document also

Document Recovery

Sometimes your system may, for one reason or another, close down before you have saved the changes to the document you were working on. The next time you start the application concerned, the Document Recovery feature will recover as much of the work you'd carried out as possible since you last saved it.

1 Open the application (in this case Word) in the usual way

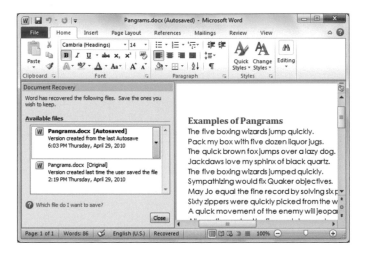

2 Check the versions of the document that are offered, and choose the one that is closest to your requirements

3 Select File, Save As, and then rename the document

Provide a different name for the autosaved version, for example, if you want to retain the original version as well.

11 Up to Date and Secure

Microsoft Update makes sure that you take advantage of updates to Office. You can also get the latest information and guidance, with online help. Office also enables you to protect your documents appropriately, and to secure your system.

Enable Updates

1 When prompted, during Office installation, choose the update option you prefer

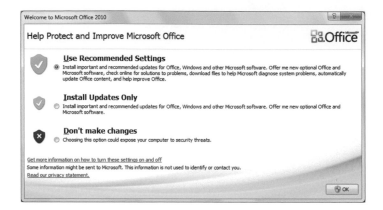

The recommended settings will provide you with updates for Office, Windows, and other Microsoft software, together with various problem-solving facilities. Alternatively, you can choose to install updates only. You can also choose not to make any changes, though this can leave your computer open to security threats.

When you choose to allow updates, these will be downloaded and applied automatically, at the preset time. However, you can request immediate updates.

2 Open an Office application, and select the File tab, and then Help and Check for Updates

3 You'll be reminded that you can also access Windows Update via the Start menu and the Control Panel

Don't forget

There's a similar process for updating Office 2010, and other Microsoft software running under Windows XP.

205

4 Windows Update locates any outstanding updates, and then offers to download and install them on your computer

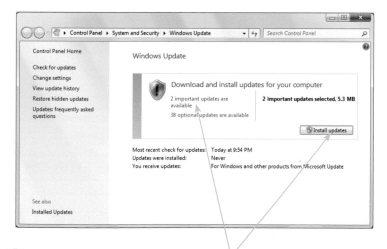

Hot tip

When you allow Windows Update to proceed automatically, these same stages will take place in the background, without any intervention required.

5 Click on the Important Updates link to see details of the updates, or select Install Updates to initiate the process

Apply Updates

1 When updates have been downloaded, Windows Update will prepare to install them

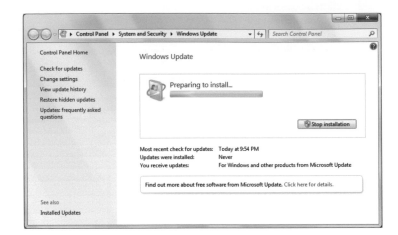

Beware

Sometimes, an update may require you to accept the associated terms and conditions before it can proceed.

2 The updates will be applied in turn. You may continue to use the system while this takes place

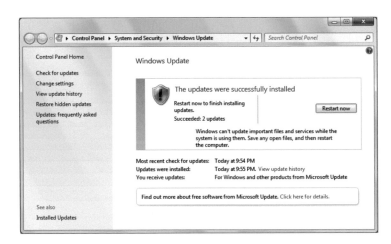

Don't forget

Windows Update will identify and download updates for all the Office applications installed on your system.

3 When updating has been completed, you may be prompted to save any open files and restart the system

4 You can select the View Update History link to see details of the updates that have been applied

Change Settings

To change the settings for Windows Update:

1 Select Start, All Programs, and then Windows Update

2 Alternatively, open Control Panel, then select System and Security and then Windows Update

3 Select Change Settings

4 Change the details for the update action, including the day or the time when updates are carried out

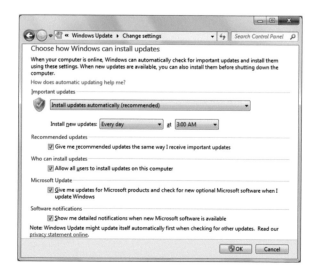

Hot tip

In Windows XP, you'd select the Start menu and the option for Microsoft Update.

Don't forget
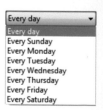

You can have Windows Update run every day, or just once a week, on a specified day.

Office Help

Don't forget

To get the latest content for Help topics, switch to the Online option, and link to the Office Online website (see page 210).

There are several ways to display Office Help for an application.

1 Press the F1 shortcut on the keyboard

2 Click the ❓ icon at the right of the tab bar

Hot tip

The Help window that opens is specific to the active application, in this case, Word, though the layout is similar for all the Office applications.

3 Select the File tab, click Help, and then select the Microsoft Office Help entry

Toolbar buttons   Title bar   Search   Close

Type words to search for

Add or remove buttons

Help topics

Help topics

Status bar

Connection status

Explore Help Topics

1 Click a Help topic to display its list of subtopics, then click one of the subtopics to display the contents

Hot tip

This shows the topic Getting started with Word, which consists of three subtopics. The content is shown for the second of these – What's new in Microsoft Office Word 2010.

2 Alternatively, click the 📖 icon (TOC button) on the toolbar to scroll through the Help topics

Don't forget

The main topics in the TOC index expand when selected, to show the subtopics. Select a subtopic, such as Quick Parts, in Creating a document, to display its description of the Quick Part Gallery.

Online Help

1 Click the Offline connection status button, and select Show content from Office.com Online

2 Help is loaded from Office.com, and the status changes, to become Connected to Office.com

3 New, up-to-date information relating to the application is now available

4 Click the arrow next to the search button to see the target search area used, offline or online

This allows you to make a temporary change, to search in a different location or area. The default connection status, and search area, will be restored, the next time you launch the application.

Developer Reference

You'll see that the Search button in Help provides a link to the Developer Reference (in both offline and online versions). This information supports the Developer tab, used mainly by users who will be developing programs, and it functions for use with Office applications. For this reason, it is normally hidden.

However, there are times when it might be useful to have access to features from the Developer tab, such as when you want to record a set of keystrokes as a macro.

To reveal the Developer tab in a particular Office application:

1   Select the File tab, then click Options and select Customize Ribbon

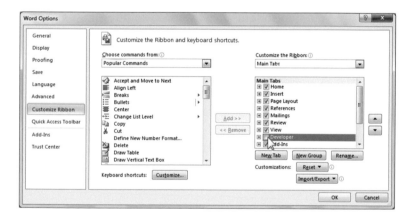

2   Click the Developer box, and then click OK

3   In Word, the Record Macro command is in the Code group. The Developer tab also includes the command groups Controls, XML, Protect, and Templates

Don't forget

Enabling the Developer tab for one Office application does not enable it in any of the other applications.

Hot tip

The groups included in the Developer tab depend on the application. In Outlook, for example, there are three groups.

Remove Personal Information

There can be more in an Office document than the information that appears when you review or print it. If the document has been subject to revision, there could be a record of all the changes, including original or deleted text and data. Any comments that reviewers may have added could still be there.

1 Select the Review tab, and click Display for Review

2 You'll see that the file contains the original text, as well the final text, each with and without the markup

Office 2010 makes it easy to completely remove such information.

1 Open the document that you wish to publish

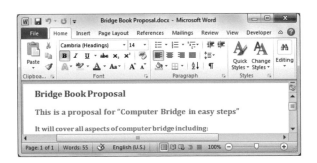

2 Click the File tab, select Save As, and enter a new file name for the document

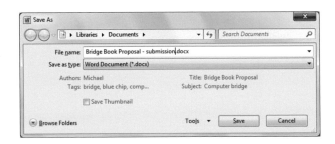

3 Click the Save button to create the working copy, which, at this stage, contains all details from the master copy

4 Select the File tab, click Info, then click the Check for Issues button, and select Inspect Document

Don't forget

You can also check for accessibility issues and compatibility issues, before making your document available.

5 Click Remove All for each item in turn, where unwanted or unnecessary data was found

Hot tip

Select those elements that may contain hidden information that you want to remove. You might allow items, such as headers, footers and watermarks, if detected.

6 When the items have been removed, click Close and save the document

Don't forget

If you've used a working copy, the information will still be available in the original document, just in case it's needed.

Protect Your Documents

Don't forget

When you send out a document, you might want to discourage or prevent others from making unauthorized changes to the content.

At the simplest level, you could tell users that the document has been completed, and should no longer be changed.

1 Open the document, select the File tab, click Info, and then Protect Document, and select Mark as Final

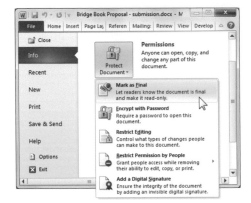

Don't forget

Another way to make the document read-only is to publish it using the PDF, or XPS document format (see page 196).

214

2 Click OK to confirm and complete the action

3 The effects of marking as final are explained

Hot tip

The commands in the groups on the Ribbon are all grayed, to show that they are unavailable for this document. The Info for the document confirms the new status.

4 This is illustrated when you next open the document. You see Read-Only on the title bar, and a warning message

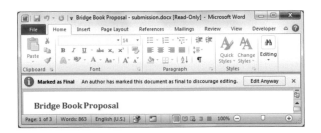

Alternatively, you might choose to encrypt the document, to prohibit unauthorized changes.

1 From Info, Protect Document, select Encrypt with Password

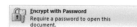

2 Provide a password for the document, click OK, then re-enter the password to confirm, and click OK again

3 The contents haven't been altered, but when you close the document, you will still be prompted to save the changes

4 Now, anyone who opens the document will be required to enter the password and click OK

If you want to remove the encryption:

5 Open the document (using the password) then select Encrypt Document, as above, delete the existing password and click OK

Restrict Permission

You can go further and apply specific levels of protection.

1 From Info, Protect Document, select Restrict Editing

2 The Restrict Formatting and Editing task pane appears

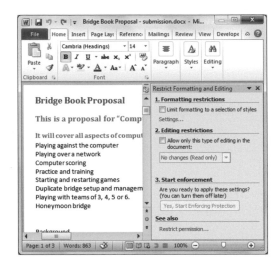

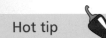
3 Choose the option to Limit formatting to a selection of styles, and click Settings, to say what styles you want in the document

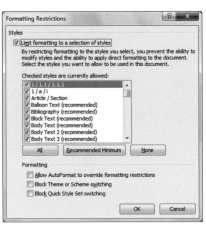

4 Choose the option to Allow this type of editing in the document, and select the level you will allow

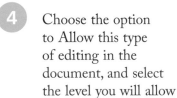

5 Click the button Yes, Start Enforcing Protection

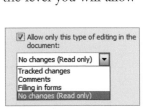

You can control online access to your documents.

1 From Info, Protect Document, select the option to Restrict Permission by People

2 You can choose Restricted Access, and then use Microsoft's Information Rights Management (IRM) service

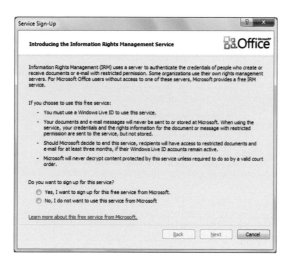

3 You'll need to register for this service, using your Windows Live ID

4 Provide the email addresses for users who are allowed to read or change the document

Finally, you can add a digital signature to your documents.

1 From Info, Protect Document, select Add a Digital Signature

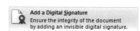

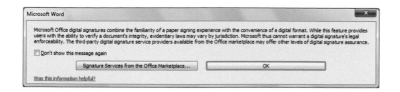

Trust Center

The Trust Center contains security and privacy settings for Office applications. To open the Trust Center and display the settings:

Hot tip

This shows opening the Trust Center from Word. It is similar for other Office applications, though the options offered may vary.

1 Select the File tab and click the Options entry, and then select Trust Center

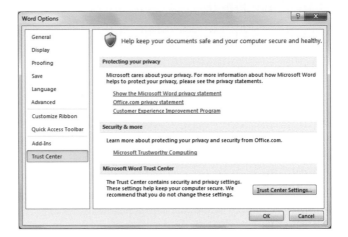

Don't forget

Click the links in the Trust Center to display information about Microsoft support, for privacy and security.

2 Click the Trust Center Settings button and choose a option, for example, Macro Settings, to see the details

Hot tip

Make changes, when required, to run macros that you create or that you receive from a reliable source, but restore settings to their original values when you've finished working with the associated document.

3 Select Add-ins to apply more stringent control over these

12 Where Next?

This provides a quick overview of other Office applications that may be in your edition, and shows you how you can use products that integrate with Office, or that share its formats. Finally, we look at using Office online, with Office Web Apps and SkyDrive folders.

Other Office Applications

Don't forget

The Office editions are:
Str   Starter
HS   Home and Student
HB   Home and Business
Std   Standard
Pro   Professional
        (and Academic)
P-P   Professional Plus
Web   Office Web Apps

We have looked at the main Office applications (Word, Excel, PowerPoint, Outlook, and OneNote) and the Office Tools in some detail, and taken a quick preview of Access and Publisher. Depending on which edition of Office you have, there may be other applications included. The editions and applications include:

Program/Edition	Str	HS	HB	Std	Pro	P-P	Web
Word	Y	Y	Y	Y	Y	Y	Y
Excel	Y	Y	Y	Y	Y	Y	Y
PowerPoint	–	Y	Y	Y	Y	Y	Y
OneNote	–	Y	Y	Y	Y	Y	Y
Outlook	–	–	Y	Y	Y	Y	–
Publisher	–	–	–	Y	Y	Y	–
Access	–	–	–	–	Y	Y	–
InfoPath	–	–	–	–	–	Y	–
SharePoint Workspace	–	–	–	–	–	Y	–
Communicator	–	–	–	–	–	Y	–

Hot tip

The version of Outlook provided with Standard and Professional Plus editions includes the Business Contact add-in.

Systems with Microsoft Office Professional Plus will have the most complete set of applications, as this Start menu folder shows:

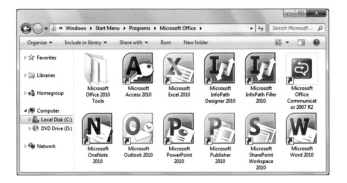

Beware

Communicator 2007 R2 is shipped with the initial release of Office 2010, with Communicator 2010 scheduled for 4Q 2010. To use Communicator you also need the Office Communications Server.

The Communicator application integrates with other Office applications, including Word, Excel, PowerPoint OneNote, and Outlook. It is designed to help the members of a group, or business, to communicate easily with others in different locations or time zones, using options like instant messaging (IM), voice and video, application sharing and file transfer.

InfoPath Designer and Filler

InfoPath is used to design, view and fill out electronic data entry forms, in XML format. It is split into two applications, InfoPath Designer to create forms, and InfoPath Filler to complete them.

InfoPath provides controls, such as Textbox, Radio Button and Checkbox. There is also Repeating Table, and other repeating controls. For each of these controls, Rules can be defined to specify actions that will be performed under certain conditions.

1. Select Start, All Programs, Microsoft Office, InfoPath Designer 2010, to select a template and create a form

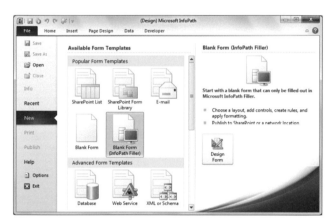

InfoPath will interoperate with SharePoint Workspace, so that forms can be completed offline and synchronized later. Forms can be imbedded into web pages, or distributed and submitted through email. You can also create a form that can only be filled out using InfoPath Filler.

2. Select Start, All Programs, Microsoft Office, InfoPath Filler 2010

3. Open the form in the shared storage, in this case a network drive

Hot tip

InfoPath forms can have fields pre-entered, entries can be validated as they are typed, and there can be links to information sources, to help fill out the details.

Don't forget

When the form has been designed, it must be published to shared storage, such as a web page, a workspace, or a network drive.

221

Beware

Using a form that can only be filled out using InfoPath Filler does, of course, mean that everyone who responds must have that product installed.

SharePoint Workspace

This program is for working on a project or report with a number of people. You set up workspaces on your computer, and share them with others. You can work offline or online, without having to worry about networks or servers, since files get synchronized.

1 Select Start, All Programs, Microsoft Office, SharePoint Workspace, and choose Create a new account

2 Select to create the account using your email address

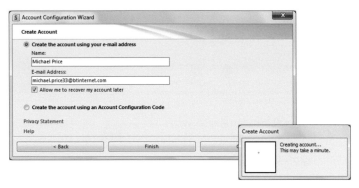

3 When the account is created, click New, Shared folder

4 Specify the shared folder name, then click Create

5 Choose the location for a new folder, or select an existing folder

6 The folder is opened and you can add or amend files, or click Share with, to give others access to the folder

7 When you next open the application, the Launchpad displays your shared folders, and allows you to add new folders, or remove ones no longer needed

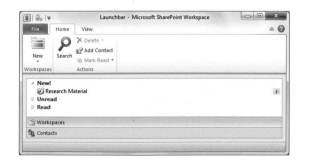

Hot tip

Your team members will have copies of the shared folder and files, and the automatic synchronization ensures that you and your team keep up–to–date.

Don't forget

SharePoint Workspace provides a list of tasks for synchronization, and for file and folder management. There's also a Chat link to communicate with the others sharing the folder.

Hot tip

For an easier way to share folders and files, use the Windows Live SkyDrive (see page 228).

More Desktop Applications

There are some desktop applications that are part of Microsoft Office 2010, but are not included in any Office edition.

Project

This is a specialized product that provides all the software tools and functions you require to manage and control a project. It handles schedules and finances, helps keep project teams on target, and integrates with other Office applications.

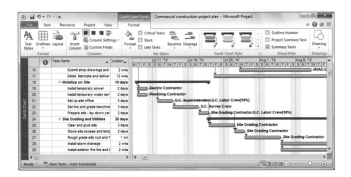

There are two versions – Standard and Professional – which add enhanced resource management, collaboration tools and project-management capabilities (supported by Office Project Server).

Visio

This is drawing and diagramming software, to help you visualize and communicate complex information. It provides a wide range of templates, including business process flowcharts, network diagrams, workflow diagrams, database models, and software diagrams, and makes use of predefined SmartShapes symbols. There are sample diagrams, with data integrated to provide context, helping you decide which template suits your requirements.

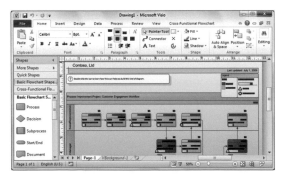

MapPoint 2010

MapPoint applications can be integrated into Office 2010 applications. There are two main MapPoint products:

MapPoint North America 2010

This includes detailed street-level maps and address find capability for the United States and Canada. There's street-level coverage (no address find) for Mexico, Puerto Rico, and US Virgin Islands. For all other parts of the world, there are just political boundaries and populated places.

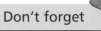
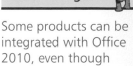

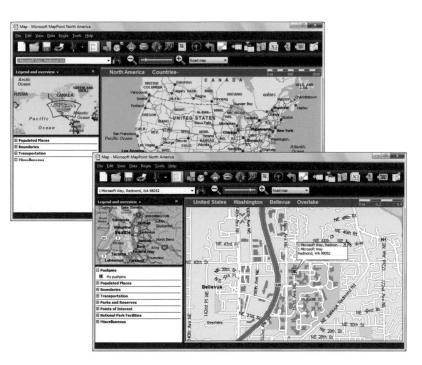

Download the free 60-day evaluation

Download and install the 60-day evaluation version of MapPoint. Note: The download file is large, so use a high-speed Internet connection.

MapPoint 2006 Europe

This has detailed street-level maps and address find capability for Austria, Belgium, Denmark, Finland, France, Germany, Greece, Italy, Luxembourg, Netherlands, Norway, Portugal, Spain, Sweden, Switzerland, and United Kingdom.

It provides some street-level coverage (but no address find) for Albania, Andorra, Bosnia and Herzegovina, Bulgaria, Croatia, Czech Republic, Estonia, France, Gibraltar, Guernsey, Hungary, Ireland, Jersey, Latvia, Lithuania, Liechtenstein, Macedonia, Isle of Man, Monaco, Montenegro, Poland, Romania, Russia, Serbia, Slovakia, Slovenia, San Marino, and Vatican City.

Using MapPoint with Office

When you install MapPoint, add-ins are installed into Office applications, so you can use MapPoint 2010 to insert maps into Office documents and presentations directly from the application. For example, to insert a map into a Word 2010 document:

1 Open the document, select the Insert tab, then click the Object button in the Text group

2 From Object type, select MapPoint Map and click OK

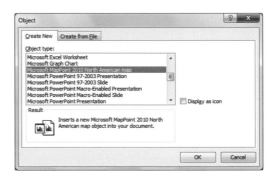

3 Locate the map section required for the document, using the MapPoint 2010 menu and toolbar, displayed here

4 Click away from the map, and the Ribbon will be restored

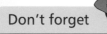
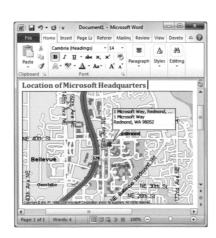

5 The map is inserted in the document

Working with Other Products

Applications that do not directly integrate with Microsoft Office will usually accept files in Office document formats, as input. For example, to place a Word document in Adobe InDesign CS5:

1 Start InDesign and open a document (new or existing)

2 Select File, Place

3 Navigate to a Word file you want to add

4 Select the document, and click Open

5 To over-ride the Word styles, create styles in the InDesign document, using the same names as the Word styles, and the text will be adjusted to use the InDesign styles when the Word document is placed

Office Web Apps

Users of any edition of Office 2010 can use Office Web Apps to share files and collaborate with other users online.

For personal use, you can access Office Web Apps via Windows Live SkyDrive (online storage). Suppose, for example, that you have a spreadsheet that you want others to view and update.:

1 Open the spreadsheet in Excel 2010

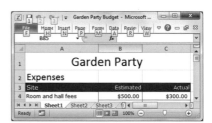

2 Select the File tab, then Save & Send, and then Save to Web

3 You'll be asked to sign in with your Windows Live ID

If you don't have an ID, select Sign up for Windows Live, and follow the prompts to create an ID (usually your email address).

4 Enter your Windows Live ID and password, then click OK

5 Your folders on Windows Live SkyDrive will be listed

6 You can save to the private My Documents, or to the shared Public, or click New to create another folder

229

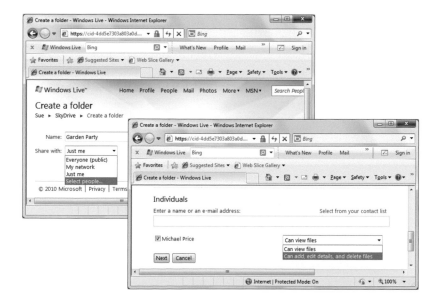

7 Specify the folder name, then say who you will share it with, and what level of access they will be allowed

Share SkyDrive Folder

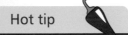

Don't forget

You can send a link later, if you prefer. You can also resend whenever you make changes to the permissions.

Hot tip

Clear the box Don't require recipients to sign in with Windows Live ID, to provide some control over access to the folder.

1 When you've created the folder, and assigned permissions, click Let People Know

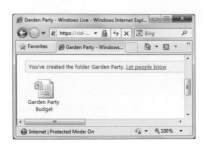

2 Type the email ID and message, then click Send

3 With the folder created, select it and click Save as, then rename (if required) and Save the file that's being shared

Access SkyDrive Folder

When the recipient opens the email, there will be a link to the shared SkyDrive folder.

Beware

Anyone who receives a copy of this email will also be able to access the shared folder.

1. Select the View Folder link

2. Sign in to Windows Live with your ID and password

3. The shared SkyDrive folder will be opened, and the files listed

Don't forget

In the shared SkyDrive folder, you can create, view, and edit files handled by one of the four Office Web Apps.

Microsoft Excel workbook

Microsoft PowerPoint presentation

Microsoft Word document

Microsoft OneNote notebook

4. Click the file you want to view, e.g. Garden Party Budget

Using Office Web Apps

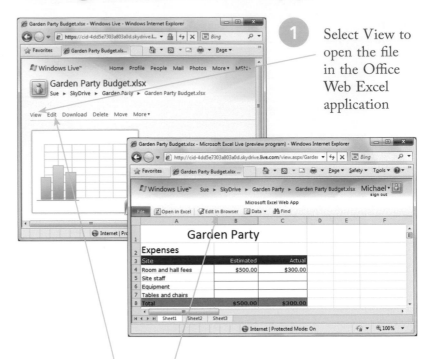

1 Select View to open the file in the Office Web Excel application

2 Select Edit or Edit in Browser to open the file, with the Tab bar and Ribbon ready for you to update and make changes

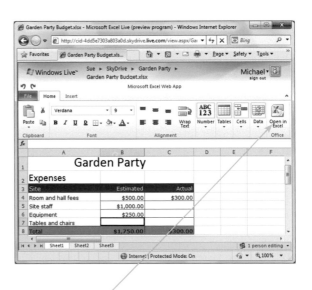

3 Select Open in Excel to view or edit the file, using the full Excel application from your copy of Office 2010

Index

235

T

U

V

W

X

Y

Z